CONTROLLED PROFITABLE GROWTH

CONTROLLED PROFITABLE GROWTH

THE ARTISTRY OF BUSINESS MANAGEMENT

PAUL F. DOUCETTE

BIZ-MANAGEMENT PUBLISHING
PACIFIC PALISADES, CA 90272

Although the author and publisher have made every effort to ensure the accuracy and completeness of information contained in this book, we assume no responsibility for errors, inaccuracies, omissions, or any inconsistency herein. Any slights of people, places, or organizations are unintentional.

First printing 2001

ISBN 09678412-4-0

LCCN 00-131712

ATTENTION CORPORATIONS, UNIVERSITIES, COLLEGES, AND PROFES-SIONAL ORGANIZATIONS: Quantity discounts are available on bulk purchases of this book for educational purposes. Special books or book excerpts can also be created to fit specific needs. For information, please contact Biz-Management Publishing, P. O. Box 1427, Pacific Palisades, CA 90272; www.doucettecorporation.com.

DEDICATION

Daryl is the love of my life. We have been married for thirty-two years. She is my number-one fan and supporter, and her love and belief in me are two of the main reasons I've been able to write this book. She conscientiously read and edited many of the early drafts of my manuscript, and her opinions have been crucial. She has always wanted the best for me. With gratitude, love, and joy, I dedicate this book to Daryl.

Proactive Selling for Profitable Growth

Epilogue

During my career I was very fortunate to have had several mentors. One of those mentors helped me to grow and develop more than the others. His name is Nathan "Nate" Landgarten. Nate simply asked questions, rather than giving answers or directives. This process was very valuable to me because I was empowered to find my own truths. He acknowledged my accomplishments, as he was not threatened by my growth. As an executive, he knew that grooming the next generation of managers was one of his most important responsibilities. Almost every good manager I have known had the positive influence of a "Nate" along the way. If you don't have a Nate in your life, get one.

Thanks to the following friends, managers, and top-notched professionals who helped tremendously by the reading of numerous drafts and offering wise counsel: Mark S. Augenstein, CPA; Neil Berlant; Denise Evans; Michael V. Glowacki, CPA, CFP, MBT; Danielle Kithcart; Mark L. Lindon, attorney; Tom Moore, attorney; Elizabeth Morgan, Ph.D.; David J. Steinhardt, MBA; and Jim Van Osdol, MBA.

Two teachers taught me more than any others. One is Tom McMillin, MFA. Tom was my professor at California State University, Northridge, when I was earning a Bachelor of Arts degree. His influence on my abilities to design and resolve problems is something I use almost every day. His high level of creativity and energy were very powerful motivational forces for me. The other teacher is Wayne Strom, Ph.D., one of my professors at Pepperdine University, where I earned my MBA degree. Wayne taught the behavioral portion of the program, and changed my behavior in a positive way forever. He helped me to see, and obtain my potential by working with me to improve my interpersonal skills. His motivational skills are truly extraordinary. He taught me and the other students how to motivate employees by first listening to desires, then teaching and coaching them how to achieve their goals. Tom and Wayne have had a very positive and powerful impact on my life.

Top-performing companies are like works of art. They are technically complex creations, usually led by masters of management. It took these experts many years to gain the knowledge they possess. If you want to be a manager, or you are a manager who wants to maximize results and master the artistry of business management, this book can help you to achieve your goals.

When I was a new manager, I wanted a book that could give me the basic information required to manage a company. I needed this book to contain information about how to properly manage the multiple functional areas that had recently become my responsibilities. Since I was a general manager, these areas of responsibility were the same as they are for most active business owners: accounting, administration, estimating, logistics, manufacturing, operations, production planning, quality, and sales. There were, and are, many excellent business books on such specific topics as accounting, distribution, manufacturing, marketing, sales, and so forth. But I was unable to find a thorough, but concise, general business book written specifically for managers. Therefore, I have written one.

Like many of today's managers, the bulk of what I've learned came from on-the-job training. Although I earned an MBA degree while working as a general manager, I learned much of what I know through experience and trial and error. One of my goals in this book is to be brief and to the point. It is written as a working tool for business managers and owners. Its purpose is to enhance your talents so that you can become a better manager and perhaps even a master of the artistry of management.

Because I've had an extremely successful career in business and my background includes diverse learning experiences, this book contains the best methods I know of for achieving controlled profitable growth. Why is *controlled profitable growth* so important? Growth, whether in sales or profits, without having the proper controls in place will eventually lead to chaos, under-performance, or even failure.

As an undergraduate, I was an art major, with an emphasis on design. I've found that there is a very close relation between good design and good business. Both require creativity, craftsmanship, focus, order, passion, spontaneity, and vision. Many managers can increase sales or profits, but doing both in a controlled way over a long period of time requires business knowledge and skill. The best managers I know, those who have *controlled* their company's *profitability and growth*, are truly artists in their work. They do in business what Rembrandt did with light, Van Gogh with color, and Picasso with creating in multiple media. Hence, I chose the title *Controlled Profitable Growth: The Artistry of Business Management.*

Management:
More Than
Just the
Numbers

Managing People: Hiring, Tailoring, Empowering, Reviewing, and Firing

Who was the best manager you ever worked for? What did he or she do to make you feel that way about him or her as your manager? This person probably earned some of your admiration and respect because he or she knew the difference between managing *people* and managing *things*.

Manage, manager, management, and *managing* are words used to describe various activities. People manage accounts receivable, accounts payable, budgets, companies, departments, inventory, plans, projects—but who manages the people? *The manager.* Being a manager is an honor, a privilege, and a responsibility. This is because unlike managing such things as accounts receivable and inventory, managing people involves making decisions that directly have an impact on their lives. When managers make more right than wrong decisions, people are hired, trained, work well, and the company grows. But when managers make a lot of bad decisions, people quit or are fired, the company becomes smaller or ceases to exist. Because decisions in business impact people's lives, they must always be made in the most thoughtful, intelligent, wise, and conscientious ways possible.

I became a general manager at the age of twenty-six. At that time, I had worked for the company for five years. It was a huge responsibility for I was now managing the employees who had been my co-workers for the last five years. I knew every employee and, in most cases, their families as well. In general, these were good, hard-

5

working people who needed their jobs to support themselves and their families. I knew the decisions I made as a new manager would directly impact the lives of the employees and their families.

To help keep this new responsibility in its important perspective, I had portrait photographs taken of all the employees who worked for the company for more than two years. (This accounted for approximately 80 percent, or approximately 70 employees.) I had the photographs enlarged to an 8-inch by 10-inch size and framed, then hung them on my office walls. When I was making important decisions, I looked at the employees' faces on my walls. This enabled me to further appreciate the impact my decisions had on their lives. It was one of my ways to remember that people were my business.

One such decision-making process involved the purchase of the company's first computer numerically controlled (CNC) machine. I understood the impact this machine would have on each of the employees because the business would dramatically change from that time forward. This was because the most skilled employees—other than the engineers and controllers—had not previously required an understanding of advanced math to perform their jobs. They were highly skilled craftspeople who made parts to aerospace industry tolerances with their abilities to read blueprints, natural talents, and years of experience. But that was about to change as the company entered the computer age.

One by one, I had to evaluate and determine how these good employees could evolve with the company. I fully explained my expectations about how the company would manufacture most of its parts in one, two, five, and ten years into the future. This led to a series of conversations with the shop superintendent, lead people, and employees to determine who wanted CNC training. As the general manager, it was my responsibility to provide training and retain as many of these good employees as possible. Fortunately, most of the good employees wanted to be trained and were successfully CNC trained. They remained to have long careers with the company.

As expensive as that first CNC machine was, it paled in comparison to the investment we had made in each other. Losing a valuable employee is one of the greatest business investment losses of all. Any person or company with money can purchase buildings, equipment, and inventory, but it is the people who are our businesses.

Hiring

If you want your company to have the right people, then as the manager you must be involved in the recruiting, interviewing, selecting, and hiring process. For medium or large companies, with more than approximately 250 employees, this is not possible or practical. Therefore, you must be certain the employees who are responsible for the hiring process meet your criteria for evaluating candidates. Unless you manage a very large company, you should be involved in the hiring process for all supervisory employees. These supervisors are your connection to the employees. They will impart your plans, messages, and visions to your company's employees, customers, and suppliers.

I like to use sports analogies for communicating examples that apply to business. A basketball team is a good example. If the five best centers in basketball were on the same team, playing in the same game at the same time, the results would be disastrous. During the game, other teams with quicker players, better outside shooters, and better ball handlers would make the five best centers appear awkward and slow. In basketball, the teams with well-balanced line-ups usually win the championships.

The same is true in business. If a company only had operational employees, more than likely the non-operational functions in the company would suffer. The same lack of balance would occur if the company were composed solely of salespeople. The company's sales would probably be at an all-time high, but the other functions would most likely be neglected. The point is, there are important reasons for each position on a team, whether in sports or in business. Make sure yours is well balanced.

Tailoring

Today it's in vogue to write lengthy job descriptions for every position in a company. I've found that one-page job descriptions are usually adequate. Business is changing so rapidly that maintaining lengthy job descriptions is generally not cost-effective. Also, it can cause your company to hire people based on obsolete standards. For most positions, you should look for a candidate who can do approximately 80 percent of the job. The remaining 20 percent should be tailored to maximize the strengths and minimize the weaknesses of the candidate. The following is an example of tailoring.

Your company has five salespeople who cover North America. You are looking for a sales manager. The ad is placed, resumes and cover letters are submitted and reviewed, and the interviewing process begins. I recommend having at least three supervisors with good people skills interview the candidates. When possible, there should be a balance of men and women in the interviewing process. I've found that men and women "read" people differently, which gives a much more complete analysis of the candidates. Also, if three supervisors do one-on-one interviews, this will give you a good idea about the candidate's capabilities and how he or she will fit into your company's culture.

In this hypothetical search for a sales manager, you, the Chief Operating Officer (COO), and the Chief Financial Officer (CFO) do the interviewing. Afterward, the three of you agree that one candidate appears to be exactly who you are looking for. But the candidate is weak when it comes to administrative details. During the interviews, the person asked if there was a sales department secretary. Your company's sales department has never had a secretary before as that function has been done by the general office staff. However, the reasons the candidate gives for requiring a secretary appear to be valid. Having a secretary would enable the sales manager to spend more time with customers, and he or she would also have more time to coach the sales force.

In your company's marketplace, a good secretary costs $35,000 per year. The sales manager requires a base of $100,000 per year, plus a performance-based incentive. This is in keeping with the other candidate's compensation requirements and is the going rate for these positions. The total annual expense, including bonuses and fringe benefits, for the sales manager and sales secretary is $175,000.

If you hire this candidate and the secretary, it will be the first time in your company's history that a department has had its own secretary. You, the COO, and the CFO agree that adding a sales secretary is the best way to support the additional administrative workload and to address the best sales manager candidate's weakness. The increased activity will be in quoting, correspondence, and preparing presentations. If you're right by selecting this candidate as your sales manager, it makes sense to assume that the administrative activity will increase. Also, this should improve customer service, as the sales secretary will be a primary inside contact for your company's customers.

On further investigation you discover your general office's output is maximized. Therefore, there is an open employee requisition for a part-time accounting clerk. Considering these valid points, you decide the potential this candidate offers your company is worth the additional expense. Furthermore, tailoring this position will allow this person to become a successful sales manager. In this example, you end up tailoring the general office's accounting clerk's position at the same time. This is accomplished by eliminating the requirement for a part-time clerk, since the sales-related work will be done by the new sales secretary.

One of the reasons the hiring process is so important is that it is directly related to your company's growth. Growth in sales means you require more employees. Decreases in sales mean you require fewer employees. As the manager, the survival of the company is your primary responsibility, because the shareholders are relying on you to protect their investments. They are betting with their pocket books that your talents will give them a better ROI than they can receive from safer passive investments, such as certificates of deposit (CDs) and federally insured bank accounts. They want their investments in safe hands. Most importantly, they never want their investments to become worth less—or worthless.

Empowering

"Empowerment" is one of the most overused, misused, misunderstood words in business. Some managers believe they have empowered their employees. They hire a person and have him or her start work on a Monday morning. That morning, the new employee fills out all the necessary paperwork. That afternoon, he or she is taken by another employee to see the facility and meet key employees. When the new hire returns to work on Tuesday, he or she has been "empowered" to do his or her job.

I wish empowering employees were that simple. Empowerment in business occurs when employees are thoroughly trained, then given the power, authority, and resources to get their jobs done right. Empowerment is about "we" and "us," not about "you" and "me."

Managers, like everyone, make mistakes. When this occurs, admit your errors in judgment and take responsibility for your actions. By doing this, you set the proper example for your employees. They can see firsthand that your actions speak louder than your words. Obviously, your employees aren't perfect either. Empowerment involves dealing with mistakes in a non-blaming way. The important thing is to learn from the mistake so it won't happen again. As a manager, the last thing you should do is create an unnecessarily stressful environment for your employees. I've found that most people don't work well in stressful environments. Empowerment is more than just a word or part of a slogan. It is a way of dealing with employees as people who are on the same team as us. When managers misuse power, they damage their employees and companies.

Reviewing

Do you want and need to know how you are performing at your job? I assume your answer is yes, and most of your employees will answer the same way. Informally, let your employees know how they're doing on a regular basis. When they do a good job, tell them. When they don't do a good job, also tell them. But do it constructively so he or she will learn from the experience. Most employees want and need recognition from their managers when they've done good jobs.

The most common complaint I hear from employees about their direct supervisor is that the supervisor never lets the employees know how they are doing—good or bad. When I hear this, I know I need to do a better job training that supervisor. If it is said frequently of the same supervisor, it makes me wonder if that person should continue being a manager. The most common response I receive from supervisors when I asked them why they didn't give their employees feedback is, "I'm too busy." This response always amazes me. How could a supervisor be too busy to evaluate his or her employees' performance? This attitude was a clear indication that I needed to retrain—or recruit!

A technique I use for recognizing good work is to write a personal note on the stub portion of the employee's payroll checks. I do this when an employee is paid a substantial sales commission or bonus. By doing this I reinforce that doing good work is directly tied to making more money. Since the payroll is usually processed every two weeks, employees earning production-based incentives could receive Thank You notes twenty-six times a year. Sales commissions are frequently paid monthly, so salespeople could receive twelve positive notes a year. When there is an exceptionally large bonus or commission, I personally hand the employee his or her check along with a thank you for a job well done.

It's also important to recognize employees for something other than commissions or bonuses—something that is uniquely about them. For this I chose sending all employees cards on their birthdays, with a personal note from me. Over the years hundreds of employees thanked me for remembering them on their special day. It's so important for a manager to let his or her employees know how important they are to the manager and to the company.

Formal reviews must be done in compliance with your company's employee handbook, and state and federal laws. I always review and have my managers and supervisors review all new employees at the end of their first ninety days with the company. This is also the end of the probationary period for all new hires. After that, I formally review all hourly employees every six months and all salaried employees annually. Why the different time intervals for salaried and hourly employees? Hourly employees usually aren't supervisors; therefore, their main responsibility is to complete a certain amount of work. Frequently, these employees have less contact with management and know significantly less about the company than the managers. The periodic review process is an effective way to keep communication open between the employees and management.

When I was a general manager, I reviewed every employee. The division had only eighty-five employees, so it was possible for me to do so. I reviewed my direct reports on a one-on-one basis. In the cases of the employees who did not report directly to me, I had their direct supervisors do the reviews with me. All reviews included what the employees did well, areas in which the employees should improve, and areas in which the employees wanted to improve.

I also asked every employee this question: "What can I do to be a better employee for you?" The first time I asked an employee this question, he looked a little shocked. I explained that one of my most important jobs is to be their best employee. I further explained that I was fortunate enough to be a manager. Being a manager meant I had the authority, power, and responsibility to make things better for them. When something was important to them, it was important to me as well. They quickly learned that I meant what I said. Not because I could resolve all of the problems, but I cared enough about them as people to do everything in my power to improve their situations. People are our business.

Manager's Evaluation Questionnaire

Several years ago I developed the following questionnaire to help me improve as a manager. I find it to be a valuable self-improvement tool.

MANAGER'S EVALUATION QUESTIONNAIRE

I am in the process of evaluating and improving my management skills. Please complete the enclosed anonymous and confidential questionnaire by _____. I have provided a self-addressed stamped envelope for your convenience. All questions should be answered by writing a number between 0 through 10 in the answer field. A 10 represents the best score, a 0 the worst.

1. When you have a problem, how effectively do I work with you to resolve it? Answer:_____

2. In dealings with you and your employees, how well do I treat you and them in terms of dignity, honesty, openness, and respect? Answer:_____

3. How clearly and consistently do I communicate our performance goals? Answer:_____

4. Do you believe I have empowered you to achieve our performance goals? Answer:_____

5. How do you perceive me as being a "hands-on" manager? Answer:_____

6. When I don't have the answer to one of your questions, how rapidly and appropriate is my eventual answer? Answer:_____

7. When I make a mistake, how rapidly and appropriately do I take responsibility? Answer:_____

8. For many years I have said there are six words that summarize our financial performance goals: "Controlled Profitable Growth" and "Return on Investment." How closely do my day-to-day actions reflect my belief in the six words? Answer:_____

9. How effectively do I lead, train, and motivate you and your employees? Answer:_____

10. What is your overall rating of me as a manager? Answer:_____

11. Comments (optional):

The completed questionnaires are extremely helpful to me. My managers and employees are also my "internal customers." I know I must continuously improve as a manager, because being as good in the future as I am today isn't good enough for me.

Firing

One of the unpleasant responsibilities of a manager is firing employees. Aside from terminating an employee for cause or when an employee voluntarily resigns, every other reason employees are terminated is caused by the manager. I know this may be difficult to believe, but it's true. When your company goes through a slow period and there is a layoff, it is your responsibility. You can say, "It's the economy," or "It's the industry we're in," but you are responsible for improving shareholders' value—no matter what! It's your job to find new and profitable markets for your company or to gain profitable market share from your competitors.

Many managers I've worked with found it was much easier to structure for growth cycles than it was to deal with downsizing. Some of them didn't know how to downsize their companies without negatively impacting customer service. They didn't know how to re-engineer or restructure their companies for lower sales. Since their company's growth in sales and employment occurred over several years, they had forgotten how to operate at a smaller size, with fewer employees. Coaching them through the re-engineering and restructuring processes often worked for me. I found that asking them how their companies were structured when they had lower sales helped tremendously.

Frequently, the managers would find old organizational charts. After reviewing them they would say; "Yeah, so that's how we did it." To help managers remember this process, I use the following phrase: Structure to match reality. When your company's business is smaller and you've tried everything you can think of to make it bigger, and you want to remain profitable, structure to match the new reality. Be flexible!

As the manager, it is your responsibility to fix employee problems and do the firing. When you make a hiring mistake, don't perpetuate the mistake by keeping the employee. It's not fair to the employee, your other employees, or your shareholders. If you don't deal with the situation promptly and properly, you jeopardize your creditability. Most employees want to feel successful at their jobs. If they are never going to feel successful while working for your company, the humane thing to do is to terminate that employee. I am painfully aware that many employees live from paycheck to paycheck. But keeping them employed denies them the possibility of finding more emotionally and financially rewarding jobs. If they are even a little resourceful, then in a reasonably short period of time, they will find jobs in which they are valued and able to feel successful.

Terminating any employee is always a serious action. Therefore, before he or she is terminated, make sure you and your management team have trained them properly and given them every opportunity to be successful. Also, make sure you or one of your managers has a one-on-one discussion with the employee that is documented in his or her file. This is to ensure that everyone understands what's wrong and what's required for the employee to remain with the company. Establish a specific date and time to review that employee's progress. This first review should be no longer than thirty days after the verbal warning meeting.

When the employee shows progress, great. If there isn't sufficient progress, give the employee a written notice. This notice may include placing the employee on probation. Set a specific date and time for the third meeting. The third meeting should take place within ninety days. At this meeting the employee should be returned to a regular employee status or be terminated. You may opt for extending the probationary period, but having an employee on perpetual probation usually only prolongs the inevitable.

Make sure your company is in compliance with all the state and federal employment laws. If your company has an employee handbook, it too must be in compliance with all state and federal laws. It is a good practice to have your company's employee handbook reviewed and approved by a labor attorney annually or as the labor laws change.

The termination of all management employees should be done by you. The exception, as with hiring, is when you manage a very large company. Then have the next highest level manager do the termination of supervisors who don't report directly to you. Always choose a time and place that works best for the employee. This is an unpleasant experience so you need to make it as professional and gracious as possible for the employee. Friday afternoons are a good time because the terminated employee has the weekend to begin to deal with this negative event.

Have all the necessary termination paperwork prepared before the meeting. Be sure you, your manager, or someone from the human resources department is there to explain the termination paperwork. This allows the terminated employee to remain in one office and not be seen by other employees while going through this stressful process. As I wrote at the beginning of this chapter: People are our business. When a person leaves your company, treat them with the same dignity and respect they received when they joined your company. Treat them as you would like to be treated under similar unfortunate circumstances.

When approximately 80 percent of the people you hire become good productive long-term employees, you and your management team are doing a good job in the hiring process. Of course, this is predicated on your company meeting or exceeding its financial and other important goals. When your company isn't achieving its goals, there is a management problem. As the manager, you must make the necessary changes to get your company back on track. When you can't, don't, or won't make the required changes, you should be replaced. This may be difficult, but sometimes the company outgrows your skills and talents. If this happens, it's better to resign or to transfer to another position within the company where you can be successful. As the manager, the last thing you should do is put your customers, employees, shareholders, and suppliers at risk. As painful as this option may seem, in the long-run it is in the best interests of everyone. You will be respected for doing what was right and necessary. Also, you can respect yourself for doing the right thing.

Summary

The Artistry of Managing People: Hiring, Tailoring, Empowering, Reviewing and Firing lies in the creation of a winning team. An example of winning teams are the New York Yankees who won the 1998 and 1999 World Series. The consensus about these Yankee teams is that there are only a couple of superstars. The remainder of both championship teams were made up of good, solid players. These players know the fundamentals, complement one another on the field, and play to win. Team manager Joe Torre received a lot of well-deserved credit for putting such an effective combination of players on the field every day and for the results they achieved. Managing people means treating them with compassion, dignity, fairness, honesty, openness, and respect. Why? *People are our business.*

Lead, Train, and Motivate

CHAPTER TWO

Leadership

As a manager, you are responsible for leading, training, and motivating your employees. Performing all three activities over a long period of time may qualify you to be a leader in the eyes of your competitors, customers, employees, shareholders, and suppliers.

Being a leader is more than being a manager. In most companies, many employees have the title of manager. Few, if any, have the title of leader. Leaders have the ability to make others perform better. They have a vision for themselves, their companies, and the employees they lead. One of the interesting characteristics about leaders is that their styles vary widely. They know what works for them and what doesn't. Leaders have mastered the art of using their skills productively and consistently on a long-term basis.

We can probably all think of people we consider leaders. Some that come to mind from the areas of business, entertainment, history, politics, and sports are Larry Bird, Sir Winston Churchill, Walt Disney, Bill Gates, Lee Iacocca, Magic Johnson, Michael Jordan, Nelson Mandela, Golda Meir, General Colin Powell, Steven Spielberg, General Norman Schwarzkopf, Joe Torre, Mother Teresa, Margaret Thatcher, Harriet Tubman, President George Washington, and John Wooden. These people have very little in common—their backgrounds, interests, and styles of leadership vary tremendously. They are, however, united by the fact that they successfully led people to excellence or to a level of production very few thought was achievable.

Leaders help people see what's possible. Successful business leaders clearly and consistently communicate their vision for the future to their employees. Some leaders and managers train their employees to develop their own visions for the future.

As a manager, a technique I use to help employees begin to create their own visions for the future is to ask a few simple questions:

- What is your vision of how you would like your area of responsibility to be performing a year from now? (The more senior the manager, the more years I ask about. For example, I might ask a general manager about the next two to three years, whereas I would ask a corporate vice president about the next two to five years.)
- What is required to make your vision a reality?
- What can I do to help you make your vision a reality?

Obviously, these are not questions you should ask your key employees every day. Choose an appropriate time and place to ask these questions. These questions should be asked and discussed during quality private times. Not all employees have the ability or desire to create a vision for their future or to become leaders. This is completely normal and perfectly acceptable. Spend your time training the employees who have the ability and desire to become leaders in your company. The better they are, the better you and your company are.

Several years ago I read an article entitled "The Boss Everyone Wants to Work For." It is a wonderful article that lists eleven traits of a great leader. I would gladly give the author credit, but I no longer have the original source. I thought so highly of the information contained in the article, I had it reduced to 3-inch by 5-inch laminated cards. I gave hundreds away to business associates, employees, and friends. I think you will find the following excerpt to be worthwhile information:

Being a good boss means being a great leader. Some leaders are born, but most are not. Leadership skills can be acquired and cultivated. Here are eleven traits of a great leader—the boss everyone wants to work for.

1. Leaders have a vision. Visualize where your organization is headed, and communicate this vision to your employees.

2. Leaders inspire employees to contribute to this vision. Employees who feel like cogs in the machinery, are unlikely to work as hard as employees who feel like valued contributors to a shared vision.

3. Leaders have high energy. Energy is infectious. If you consistently radiate energy, your employees are bound to catch some of your rays.

4. Leaders are supportive. By finding areas where your employees' goals overlap your organization's goals, you can support both the individual and your organization at the same time.

5. Leaders are not afraid to lead. Being a good leader means exerting some control over employees' lives. If you are uncomfortable doing this, your leadership abilities will be blocked.

6. Leaders take the time to lead. Don't just put your nose to the grindstone and never look up. Take the time to give praise, to offer and solicit constructive criticism, and to communicate your vision.

7. Leaders are communicators. Develop your reading, writing, speaking, and listening skills.

8. Leaders are decisive yet flexible. Be decisive when setting goals. But when working toward these goals, don't be afraid to change the tactics if necessary.

9. Leaders are problem solvers, not blame assignors. No matter how strong a leader you are, things will go wrong. When they do, it is important not to waste time blaming people. Instead, work toward solving the problem.

10. Leaders get down in the trenches. Do not adopt a double standard. If you expect extra work from your employees, you must be willing to do extra work yourself.

11. Leaders demand excellence. If your employees know that you think them capable of excellence, they will feel inspired to strive for excellence.

If you are the boss, the chances are you have already acquired leadership skills. But there is always room for improvement.

If you are a good leader, work to become great. If you are great, work to become the greatest!

There is another important thing to remember about being a leader. The title of leader is given by others when they talk about a person, not by the person saying, "I am a leader." Leaders show with actions and words that they are worthy of the highest title any manager can be given—that of a leader.

Training

I am a big believer in training the trainers. Spend time and money training your managers and supervisors. Unless your company has a job requirement for a specific skill, the majority of supervisors' training should be done by you. You may be thinking, "I'm not a teacher!" That's okay—do it anyway! Choose a topic you know a lot about, and one your managers and supervisors want to learn about as well. Then develop a lesson plan for that topic. Start small, keeping the first session to around two hours. If your employees learn from you and you enjoy teaching, try it again. If it doesn't work after a couple of tries, then hire the best professional trainer you can find.

The reason I'm suggesting you first try teaching your employees is because many managers are good trainers. It may be a talent you possess, even though you never had any formal training. Also, your employees will appreciate and enjoy the personal attention you are giving them. In turn, you can become more than just an "order giver," because training others increases your ability as a "solution provider." Then have your managers train the employees who report to them. Again, this is based on their abilities to teach well. This type of learning is a two-way street. I found I learned as much, if not more, from my employees than I believe they learned from me. I believe all of our lives were enriched through this process.

All employees should be trained in Total Quality Management (TQM). TQM is a methodology that provides employees with the tools to operate the company on a continuously improving basis. The three main principles of TQM are Employee Empowerment (EE), Statistical Process Control (SPC), and Just-In-Time (JIT).

- EE is achieved when all employees have full participation in resolving problems and controlling the company's quality.
- SPC means all employees have been given statistical training for measuring the quality of their own work.

- JIT inventory involves using production methods that use small quantities of parts that are delivered directly to the actual manufacturing or assembly point-of-use (POU). This is in contrast to large inventories maintained in warehouses that are subsequently delivered to a production control department, and then delivered to the POU.

The ultimate goal of TQM is zero defects, although many quality experts do not express the goal of TQM as zero defects. This is because most processes are not robust (repeatable) enough to produce every transaction or part within specifications. Therefore, the practical goal of TQM is continuous improvement. Properly implemented TQM will create practices and attitudes that can make your company best-in-class (the best company as compared to your peers).

People learn in different ways. Some learn by reading, while others learn from attending a seminar, taking a class, or majoring in a subject. For important and long-lasting gaining of knowledge, many people learn by observing and listening to others, and through their own life's experiences. Find out what methods work best for your employees as individuals, not as a group. When there is a topic that interests several of your employees, then group training is fine, provided it's effective. When you know the employees well, you probably know what method of training works best for each of them.

The problem with group training is that what works best for each employee, won't work best for all employees. Herein lies the inherent problem with group training, but sometimes it is the most pragmatic approach. When this is the case but you don't know what methods will work best for most of your employees, ask them. Take the time to talk with each employee to determine what methods should be used. If you discover that one method is consistently suggested, great! If not, allow the employees to design their training sessions. By doing this, you have empowered them to create their training program, which can generate very positive results.

As stated earlier, your key managers should be developed and trained by you. This does not mean you are expected to know everything about business. What this does mean is that you should be a resource and mentor in the training of your managers. Do this in ways that lets them know how important their growth is to you. Your personal involvement in your key employees' growth will give them the recognition they deserve.

Some time ago, I trained a newly promoted general manager of a highly complex contract manufacturing division. Once I was the general manager of this same division. The division's business was booming, so during the day there was little time for training. After a few very frustrating days with constant interruptions, we decided to change our training plans. To achieve our training goals, we met every day for half an hour before and after the division opened and closed. This training involved walking the shop floor while discussing the capabilities of every piece of equipment. We also took this time to discuss which employees were qualified to operate the various pieces of equipment. We also discussed the various part's operational sequences and what to look for regarding proper and improper material handling. With few exceptions, we had our two daily training sessions for six months. By the end of the sixth months, the new general manager knew most of what I knew about the division and had acquired knowledge from his own experiences. This method of training took a tremendous commitment from both of us. But it was the best method we knew for accomplishing what we needed to do.

For ongoing informal business training, I gave business articles and books to the employees with whom I worked. I found this is stimulating for those employees who learn by reading. These employees appreciated this approach to learning because it stimulated ongoing discussion about new information, while creating an atmosphere of learning. Some employees are more likely to learn by watching a video in the comfort of their homes. There are business videos on many topics, and they can be an excellent training resource.

New ideas are constantly generated in and out of the business world. No manager can possibly know the answers to every business question, maximize every opportunity, or resolve every problem. Therefore, an essential part of many successful companies is having ideas come from various sources. And these sources of inspiration can come from anywhere. Keep your eyes and ears open, while allowing the ideas—usable or unusable—to flow. The ongoing stimulus a learning environment creates can foster new and better ideas that will keep your company ahead of the competition.

One of your main functions as a manager is to maximize every opportunity. This is easier to achieve when the working environment allows your employees to reach their potential. Coaching, mentoring, teaching, and training employees to achieve their goals is one of the most rewarding aspects of being a manager. An important characteristic that allows your company to successfully grow is the ability of your employees to grow as well. When your employees are given the opportunity to continuously improve, your company's improvement is much easier to achieve.

Motivation

In 1968, while attending college, I started working as a temporary part-time truck driver. In 1981, I was promoted to a corporate vice president for the same company. This promotion occurred after working thirteen years at a division, with the last eight years as a general manager. I had done every job at the division, except controller. My first assignment as a vice president was to manage a group of contract manufacturers. I was comfortable with all aspects of my new position because of my hands-on experience. But immediately after assuming my new responsibilities, I had an uncomfortable feeling that took me a while to identify.

Every month I visited each division to review the financial statements with the general manager. We discussed the results, opportunities, and problems. Then I visited every department in the division. During these visits I spoke with the employees and did a quick visual review of the work-in-process (WIP) inventory. While meeting with the general managers, I made sure their questions about the financial statements were answered thoroughly. It usually took a few monthly meetings before the general manager was comfortable with all the financial information.

I also made an assessment of the general manager's strengths and weaknesses. After each visit, either in my car or during the plane ride home, I felt an inexplicable emptiness. Something was missing. One day I realized what was causing my feelings of failure.

I remembered that during my first few years as a general manager, there was a corporate vice president who would periodically stop by on his way home from the corporate office. His name was Rudy Hummes. From a company reporting standpoint, Rudy did not have responsibility for my division. The sole purpose of his visits were to see how I was feeling as a new general manager. We would sit at the table in my office and talk over coffee or a soft drink. Rudy was a real people-person. When we spoke, I felt what I was saying was genuinely important to him. Our talks didn't last very long—an hour at the most. We never reviewed my division's financial statement. We just talked about what was important to me. When my conversations with Rudy ended, I walked him to the door and said goodbye. Then I returned to my office and realized I felt like a million bucks! This was because Rudy had motivated me with his caring attitude about me.

While I was a general manager, I earned an MBA degree. As part of the program I wrote a thesis, *Meeting With Low-Producing Employees and Its Effect on Their Productivity*. Some of the inspiration for my thesis came from these positive experiences with Rudy. What I learned from Rudy, other role models, and my own experiences was that talking with employees about their issues was very important and meaningful to them. Also, it was one of the best ways for us to feel connected. It was a way to make managing employees more human. Business is more than managing numbers. It is about developing important long-term relationships, working with people, and doing good work.

Writing the word "work" reminded me of seeing a televised interview of Sir Laurence Olivier several years ago. The interviewer asked him a typical question he was probably asked hundreds of times before: How would you like to be remembered? His answer was far more interesting to me than the routine question, because I had assumed I knew how he would answer. Instead of answering with something about his great acting ability, he said something about being remembered as a "perfectionist worker." I was so taken with his humility, his answer left an everlasting impression on me as to how I view work and workers. Work is a good thing. Good workers are a very good thing. Perfectionist workers are a better thing.

Throughout this book I use the term "employee" to describe people who are paid to do work. I am aware that the term "team member" is more correct for many business people. There is nothing wrong with being an employee. There is wrong in not doing the best work you can.

These recollections of how Rudy made me feel helped me to understand what was missing during my monthly meetings with the general managers. I was doing a good job with training, but I wasn't taking the time for the important person-to-person part of being a manager. Therefore, I wasn't motivating the managers or their employees and certainly didn't qualify as their leader.

Over the years I have trained a lot of managers. I always tell them as a manager, you must lead, train, and motivate your employees every day. I also tell them that the artistry of management is doing all three functions, in a productive way, over their entire careers. Then I tell them about Rudy. Being like Rudy, in this regard, is not an easy task. Until it became second nature to me, I had to remind myself to lead, train, and motivate my employees every time I met with them. Rudy passed away in 1980. To this day whenever I think of him, I fondly and gratefully remember how he took the time to motivate me. In the process, he not only taught me how to be a better manager, he enriched my life as well.

Summary

Mastering the artistry of leading, training, and motivating is attained when you are known as a leader by your competitors, customers, employees, and shareholders. One of the ways you'll know when you have led, trained, and motivated your employees properly is when they realize that their only failure is not to try. This is not to say everything they do will be done right. It won't. But because you have trained and motivated them properly, they will make the right decisions most of the time. Most importantly, when they make a mistake they will have learned from the experience and will apply that knowledge to future situations. Making your company an industry leader is much easier when you have mastered the artistry of leading, training, and motivating your employees.

The Board
of Directors

Every company's shareholders should be represented by a board of directors—not a board of no direction. All legal entities that are corporations have a board of directors (board). In both public and private corporations, the board hires the company's management for the primary purpose of maximizing shareholder value. The board is the company's reviewing body for the management's performance. When a company's management is not performing, it is the responsibility of the board to replace some, or all, of the company's senior level management. If the board does not replace the underperforming senior managers, the board should be replaced. The board can be replaced by a vote of the shareholders. When the shareholders vote for an existing board for another term and the company's results are consistently below that of its peers, they are allowing the poor performance to continue.

When a company is structured and performing properly, often it's because there is an appropriate balance of power between its board, management, and shareholders. This balance of power is one of the cornerstones of proper functioning governments as well.

Much as the U.S. Constitution creates a balance of power between the executive, legislative, and judicial branches of government, corporations have bylaws that dictate their balance of power. Just as each of the three governmental branches has separate duties and authorities, corporate bylaws define who has the authority and responsibility to do the various functions within a company. A company's shareholders are like a country's voting age population. Every share of common stock gets one vote. However, unlike the democratic one vote per registered voter, in a company the shareholders with the most shares get the most votes.

There are various external federal organizations that have power over companies: the Internal Revenue Service (IRS), the Securities and Exchange Commission (SEC), and the Environmental Protection Agency (EPA), are familiar examples. Internally, the major watchdog group responsible for maintaining the balance of power for the shareholders is the board of directors. The shareholders vote for a company's board, then the board hires the company's management. The board also approves the ways in which the company's management uses its major resources. Major capital expenditures require board approval. There is no single dollar limit rule for capital expenditures requiring board approval, as every company's bylaws are different. Most importantly, the board must use its authority to maintain a company's balance of power, wherever it is required.

The board members must be among the company's most valuable resources. What is required to be a good board member is very similar to what you will read in chapter nineteen about salespeople: Good board members direct. A board member must add value to the company by directing its major investments and overall business strategy. "Directing" does not mean "managing." It means reviewing and approving the management's strategic plans, and then "monitoring" the results in relation to those plans. These major investments and strategies involve every aspect of a company: community involvement, customers, employees, equipment, markets, people, plant, property, shareholders, suppliers, and technology. The board members' active participation in directing the company will improve its ability to successfully survive and prosper in the future.

When possible, it is advisable to have the majority of the company's board members be "outsiders." An outside board member is not a member of the company's management team. Board members must be objective in their actions. When they are members of the company's management, they are by definition involved in the day-to-day running of the company. This closeness to the company may make it difficult for them to be objective. Also, the board's management members have a vested interest in perpetuating their positions in the company. One of the shareholder's safeguards against this condition is utilizing a board made up of objective and highly qualified outsiders.

If a company's results are the direct responsibility of the Chief Executive Officer (CEO), then dealing with a CEO's poor performance is the direct responsibility of the board. As an interesting exercise, investigate under-performing public companies in which senior management is a majority of the board's composition. Then, research the companies in which senior management and outside board members do not own a majority of the company's common stock. I've done this on several occasions, and have been amazed at the number of poorly performing public companies that retain their current management and board. Many shareholders vote with their pocketbook: They sell their under-performing stocks, and with every seller, there is a corresponding buyer. This often leads to a perpetuation of the company's inferior board and management as the value of the shares continues to decline.

After the management and board have approved how a company's major resources can be used, the cash and lines of credit are used to fund the business cycle and fixed asset purchases. A company's business cycle must provide excellent customer service. The business cycle and customer service are discussed in chapter nine.

Summary

The artistry of selecting board members involves finding people who will add value to the company by maximizing shareholder's value. Board members must have business savvy, common sense, creativity, experience, independence, integrity, and intelligence. When you are the CEO of a public company, you must have a board who can, and will, replace you if you perform poorly. Knowing you are accountable to the board is one of the "acid tests" for every good manager.

Accountants, Attorneys, and Other Important Professionals

A young entrepreneur recently asked for my advice about the best way to start a new business. I gave him my words of wisdom about starting a business and asked him if he had a good business attorney and accountant. He indicated that he had a good accountant but was in need of an attorney. I gave him the name and telephone number of my business attorney, along with several examples as to why retaining a good business attorney is mandatory. This is because when you don't have the proper legal foundation for a business, you are building it on an unstable base, thus increasing the chances of problems. The young entrepreneur called my attorney and got a quote for forming an S Corporation (a form of the general corporation that has special tax status with the IRS in many states). The new businessman felt the price quoted was more than he wanted to spend, so he decided to do the work himself along with a paralegal friend. He called me and proudly said, "I was able to form my corporation for only $150."

To make a long, sad story short, several months went by and he had the opportunity to receive a major infusion of cash from an investor. Verbally, a deal was reached and his corporation's documentation was sent to the investor's business attorney. To the shock and disappointment of the young entrepreneur, the filing of his corporation had been done incorrectly. In fact, he had filed for C Corporation (a general corporation) status but had done that inaccurately as well, so he was really operating with no corporation at all.

31

Because of this, and the potential liability to him and the new investor, a new corporation needed to be formed. All of this was so overwhelming to the new businessman, he pulled out of the deal in frustration.

The young entrepreneur had worked so hard to start his business, only to find out he was in a less-than-zero position. Good business opportunities don't come along that frequently. He missed his first good opportunity and is now left with building his company at a much slower pace—if he can survive the high cash demands of a startup company. The lesson to be learned from this is to know when you require the help of a professional.

The term "professional" in this chapter applies to accountants, attorneys, and professional consultants. Many large companies require large professional firms, especially if they have many locations around the country or the world. However, it has been my experience that most small and medium-sized companies are better off using small and medium-sized professional firms. Some professionals with large firms may tell you that having a junior professional do some of your work is more cost-effective. I have not found this to be the case. Junior professionals have lower billing rates, but it usually takes them more time to do their work. Also, you still pay for the senior professional's time, because they must review, and in some cases re-do, the junior person's work.

No matter what size professional firm you choose, there are several very important points you want to make sure are perfectly clear. The firm you retain will have a partner or principal do your company's work. Make sure the professional has sufficient contacts in his or her field to be able to act as your "quarterback" in the event a specialty professional, such as a litigator, is required. They must be capable of directing the specialty professionals. This means they are involved in selecting, negotiating, and coordinating the overall strategy with the specialty professional. By filling this important role, the generalist professional helps you achieve your desired results.

Any firm you retain should have a minimum of two partners or professionals. The reason for this is what I call the "Mack Truck Theory." If something happens to the professional who is your primary contact—like being hit by a Mack truck—you need another professional who can handle your matters. You don't want to be in the middle of a critical situation and find yourself scrambling for professional help. However, if this unfortunate circumstance occurs, you should not be charged by your existing firm for bringing the other professional up to speed about your issues.

Another problem for managers of small and medium-sized companies is knowing when they require outside help. In other words, how do you know what you don't know? In general, unless your company has an employee who is an industry expert, you will probably benefit from an outside professional for complex problems. The business world is so complex and changes so rapidly, it is practically impossible for the employees of small and medium-sized companies to stay abreast of all the latest developments.

As a manager, you must be aware of the important trends that may impact your company. This means you should read business magazines and books, attend business seminars and industry trade shows, conduct research on the Internet, and have a network of business people as resources on an ongoing basis. This is essential if you want your company to stay ahead of the curve and not fall behind your competition.

Finding a good professional consultant can be difficult. I've found one way to accomplish this is to first see examples of their work. When you like what you've seen, make an appointment to interview the consultant. For example, say your company is going to upgrade your distribution center (DC). Make arrangements to tour customers and suppliers you believe have the best DCs. When one of the DCs is what you want for your company, find out who was the designer, equipment provider, and installer. One firm may have provided all the services, but as I write in chapter ten, don't contract with a company that has a built-in conflict of interest. Another approach is to contact managers of world class companies about touring their facilities. Tell them why you want to see their DC, and if your company is not a direct competitor, I've found most company's managers are very cooperative. In this example, you should contact the company's COO or vice president of operations, as they usually know the most about DC operations.

The initial meetings with professionals should be at no charge. This is because they are selling you on the advantages of using their services. As stated in chapter ten regarding computer consultants, always attempt to negotiate a fixed-fee arrangement with a professional. This may not be possible, as some situations don't lend themselves to fixed-fee arrangements. But there's no harm in asking.

When your company does use outside professionals, charge all of their expenses to the specific project or service.

Many professional relationships are considered confidential, and in some cases even privileged. This may make doing a reference check difficult so ask them how they recommend you do a reference check on them. Also check with their professional associations to determine if they are a member in good standing or have had complaints filed against them. Professionals survive and get new business based on their reputations. Ask business and professional people you respect about the professional you are considering. As with everything else I have discussed in this book, you must satisfy yourself when making an important business decision about the selection of a professional to represent your company.

The Internet has many powerful search engines that can help with most research. I use the following search engines for some of my research:

- *Business Week* Online (www.businessweek.com)
- *Fortune* (www.fortune.com)
- Hoover's Online (www.hoovers.com)
- MetaCrawler (www.metacrawler.com)
- Morningstar (www.morningstar.com)
- PartesFreeEDGAR (www.freeedgar.com)
- Quicken (www.quicken.com)
- S&P's (Standard and Poor's) Home (www.personalwealth.com)
- Charles Schwab (www.schwab.com)
- Value Line (www.valueline.com)
- Yahoo (www.yahoo.com)

Summary

The artistry of managing professionals for your company is in selecting the best firm and person who will do your company's work for the lowest total cost. This does not mean at the lowest billing rate. Many times the higher billing rate is more than covered by the value the higher paid professional adds to your company. You are buying experience, IQ, and specific knowledge. This is a case where you usually do get what you pay for.

The Lead
Theory

The Lead (led) Theory is a term I use that means being persistent. All of your experiences, intelligence, knowledge, and talents are valuable when you use them to do real work. As the company's manager, your willpower can determine the success or failure of many projects.

From 1983 through 1988, I attended annual meetings hosted by the management of Motorola's Semiconductor Group for its distributors. These meetings were held to discuss Motorola's managers' plans for the upcoming year and to review what their distributors required to gain market share. Many of the distributors were very guarded with information about their companies because we were in a room filled with our competitors.

There was one exception. Every year the same senior executive from a distributor spoke to the group about his company. During his presentation he explained his company's vision, strategy, and plans for the next three years. After listening to his first presentation, I pulled him aside during the cocktail hour to ask him why he was comfortable sharing this information with his competitors. His answer was, "Many managers are great at creating ideas, good at developing plans, and terrible at implementing." Unfortunately, I've found what he said is frequently true. Implementation requires persistence. Managers must stick with their plans until their projects are completed. The exception to this is when the design and plan are flawed, and therefore require modification or elimination.

There are some simple techniques and tools that can help to complete important projects on time. I use an Action Item List (see pages 150 and 179) for project management. Before the days of the personal computer (PC) and personal digital assistant (PDA)—also referred to as a "palm" type or "hand-held" device—I maintained these lists manually. Since 1990 I've used a PDA to track all my projects. These items stay in the "to do" file until they are completed. I prefer using a PDA instead of a laptop PC, because of its light weight, battery life, and small size, which allows me to have it with me at all times. However, the best of both devices can be achieved by using the 3Com Palm Pilot, the Handspring Visor, or multifunction "smart" cell phones. These little devices are smaller than a deck of cards and allow you to upload or download data to and from your PC.

Why are some goals met ahead of schedule and below budget, while others goals are late and over budget? This is a complex question with a number of possible answers. However, I believe there are two answers that are generally accurate. The first answer has to do with the complexity of the project. This is especially true when the project is not only complex, but your employees have never implemented a similar project. When a project is done for the very first time, the employees are attempting to complete it in uncharted waters. The obvious analogy is Christopher Columbus' voyage in search of a faster way to Asia. Columbus' project could only be designed and planned to the limit of available knowledge. Often "cutting-edge" companies find themselves in the same situation. This is why they are frequently referred to as "bleeding edge" companies.

The second reason is that management did not get the buy-in from the employees in order to receive their most productive support for the project's design, plan, or method of implementation. When this happens, there is some degree of mutiny occurring, and this may be because the manager is the "Captain Bligh" type. Perhaps the wrong employees were hired to do the project or were inadequately trained. It could also be a combination of these elements.

Sometimes the company's management and employees start a project in total agreement, but when the project is underway, someone discovers that something is wrong. No matter who discovers the problem, you should immediately address it. You and your employees share the common goal of completing the project on time and within budget. This can still be achieved through teamwork. As the manager, review your employees' plans to accomplish their individual tasks well before the due date. When an employee's task is falling behind schedule, do a Gap Analysis (see pages 63 and 184) and develop an Action Item List. For major projects, have them use the Design, Plan, Make, Measure, and Analyze Process (described in chapter seven).

For all of my adult life, I have always thought of myself as an above-average designer and problem solver. The two, designer and problem solver, really go hand-in-hand. Sometimes, no matter how well I've designed something and no matter how much "lead" I apply to the problem, I get stuck. About twenty years ago, I developed a process to help me get unstuck. Here's what I do: In the center of an 8½-inch by 11-inch blank white piece of paper, I write the one word or single phrase that best describes what I want to accomplish. Then, in a clockwise spiral pattern, I write all the words that come to mind, as fast as I can get them on the paper. I space the words about a half inch apart, encircle each word, and attached it to the next word's circle with a straight line. Most of the time this process works, because it allows me to view the information more objectively, sequentially, and in a relatively short period of time—usually less than five minutes.

Sometimes, however, even this doesn't work. When that happens, I take my pencil or pen from my right hand, switch it to my left hand, and continue the process. To date, this process has always worked for me.

I've read a number of books and spoken to many of my friends who are medical doctors about the functions of the right and left sides of the brain. I believe what occurs when I change writing hands is that a different portion or side of my brain starts working on the problem. The physiological explanation for this is fascinating, but all I know is that it works for me. The next time you find yourself stuck in the middle of solving a problem, try switching your pencil, pen, or mouse from one hand to the other and see what happens!

Summary

The artistry of using the Lead Theory begins with persistence. Do the best you can every day and fight for what you believe in. Many projects are very complex and require your best management skills to complete. When the project is worthwhile, keep at it, and don't get discouraged or lose focus because it's taking a long time to complete. Quite often, good things do take a long time to complete.

Having Fun

When you truly enjoy your work, you'll be happy in your job most of the time. For most managers I know—and for myself—this means you enjoy working with people. As a manager, almost everything you do involves working with others. Some people prefer working alone, but because they did their jobs so well, they were promoted to a managerial position. Sometimes, people can be trained to be a manager. Other times they can't. The people who can't be trained to be managers are the ones we see doing what they used to do most of the time, rather than leading, training, and motivating their employees.

Here's an example: A staff accountant is promoted to CFO but instead of assuming his or her role as a manager, he or she still does the detailed accounting work. Often, these "managers" hang out in their offices, deeply engrossed in doing something alone. I find this to be very sad, because if you look at their faces, you rarely see a smile. They have been promoted out of their element of dealing with inanimate objects to dealing with people.

I've spoken with thousands of people and read numerous articles about people's monetary compensation in relation to their job satisfaction. For most of these people, their compensation isn't what allows them to enjoy their jobs. Their earnings are usually somewhere in the middle or lower half of what's important to them about work. Ahead of their earnings are usually such items as the task itself, recognition, co-workers, growth potential, security, responsibility, and authority. A certain amount of pay is obviously necessary and important to most of us. But does it make us happy at our work? I don't think so.

I had a brother in-law named Joe Carter, now deceased, who loved working on cars. His job involved working on cars. Joe could be found in his garage working on cars many evenings and weekends too. Just give Joe a car to work on and he was happy. Some of his work was not of the highest quality, but that didn't matter to Joe. He loved what he was doing so much, he got tremendous enjoyment from just working on cars. He was one of the happiest, most successful, and most satisfied people I've ever known. Joe had fun doing his work almost every day.

Another very important personal achievement is having balance in your life. Mother Nature has provided the planet with gravity so we all know the physical importance of being balanced. But the non-physical world is abstract and requires self-evaluation to determine whether or not one's life is in balance. An out-of-balance condition in one part of a person's life usually leads to trouble in the other parts. All work and no play, or all play and no work, are out-of-balance conditions. Unfortunately, there is no simple answer as to what is the right balance for we are all individuals with different wants and needs. I truly believe you should deal with an out-of-balance condition as if you were bitten by a rattlesnake, because it can be that poisonous. The people I know who dealt with their out-of-balance conditions head-on dramatically improved their lives. They were also able to have more fun!

Being a manager involves doing tasks that aren't fun, but they're your responsibility. What you do most days should be fun and rewarding, or it will become old and pure drudgery within a very short period of time. I've found that when people are able to make money doing what they love to do, they are usually financially and personally successful. If you don't enjoy what you do for work, give some serious thought to changing careers. Life is too short to spend forty, fifty, or sixty hours a week doing something we don't enjoy.

During my thirty-plus years as a manager, many young employees and managers asked me how they know if they have selected the right career. I answered them by saying: Always follow love. I've found when most people do what they love for their careers, it makes them happy, at peace, and successful. They may not be the wealthiest people from a monetary standpoint, but they enjoy some of the riches of life money can't buy.

Summary

The artistry of having fun lies in loving what you do for work most days. When something good is happening, allow yourself to feel and appreciate the pleasure of that experience. Find something you love doing. When you are able to do what you love, you will be successful and happy in your career.

Planning, Profitability, and Resources

Strategic Business Planning: The Design, Plan, Make, Measure, and Analyze Process

The quickest way to accomplish a business goal is by doing what is the most direct and economical. Therefore, I created the Design, Plan, Make, Measure, and Analyze Process to achieve excellent results—quickly and efficiently.

As an undergraduate student I was an art major with an emphasis on design. The development of this process is one of the best examples of how I use my artistic and business backgrounds simultaneously. My need to develop this process came from my training experiences with employees, managers, and supervisors. To successfully start, manage, and finish any project or business venture, I recommend doing the following five functions in order:

1. Design
2. Plan
3. Make
4. Measure
5. Analyze

In the following hypothetical example, you are the manager and owner of an industrial distributor. I am using one hypothetical example because it allows me to explain the process more clearly. However, this example is based on using this process in numerous actual situations, over the course of three decades.

Design

The design process is the first step in doing a project, creating a product, or starting a business. To achieve the desired result, you must start with a pure design. The purer the design, the less time and money are required to accomplish your goal. The design must address five fundamental elements: who, what, when, where, and why. The answers to these five questions are your Opportunity Statement. (For many years I referred to this as a Problem Statement. Now, I use the term Opportunity Statement, because it more accurately describes the circumstance.)

1. Who: Your company is an industrial distributor based in Los Angeles. It is a well-established, single-location distributorship with annual sales of $60 million, earnings before interest and taxes (EBIT) of $6 million, and a 20 percent market share.

2. What: Grow your company's EBIT, return on investment (ROI), and sales while improving customer and supplier relationships.

3. When: This expansion must to be completed in six months.

4. Where: You and your management team are beginning an expansion project into a new marketplace within the western region.

5. Why: In the recent past, several customers have relocated from Los Angeles to smaller cities in the western region because these cities have lower costs of living and more qualified workforce pools. Los Angeles is one of the most competitive marketplaces in the country. Growth is necessary for the long-term success of your company, as this industry is consolidating. Doing a good job in one city is no longer considered enough to be a sales and market share factor by the customers and suppliers. After taking all of this into consideration, you must ask yourself what you and your employees would do to successfully enter a new marketplace.

Risk

One way I view the significance of major projects is by using the analogy of going to battle in a war. Whatever you do, your company can't go out of business (die) while expanding into a new marketplace (battleground). To ensure the worst-case scenario doesn't become a reality, and before you do anything, determine what resources are available for this expansion. In business, resources are money, people, and time. They are always "finite" amounts, not "infinite." Therefore, determine how much capital your company can have "at risk" for this new venture. "At risk" asks the question: If the expansion is a total failure and every expenditure is a total loss, can your company afford the loss?

People

When your company can afford the risk, select the best available people who can help make this a successful venture. If you find that the best people already work for your company, how will their absences impact the Los Angeles location? Next, determine how much time will it take the new location's employees to generate an acceptable EBIT, ROI, sales, and market share. After determining "what" you want your company to achieve and "when" you want to achieve it, you have the two elements of your new location's pro forma (projected) financial statement.

ROI Targets

As a criterion for evaluating potential investment, I've seen managers set ROI targets as low as 15 percent and others higher than 100 percent. Establishing a target and then achieving the ROI, depends to a large extent on the type of company and industry. It is very difficult for a company to achieve an 85 percent ROI, when the industry average is only 20 percent. When a distributor's cost of money is 10 percent or less, a target ROI of 25 percent is usually satisfactory. (Note: Throughout this book, the term "distributor" refers to dealers, fulfillment companies, and master distributors.) Manufacturers typically have ROI targets of 35 percent or more when their cost of money is also 10 percent or less. When the cost of money to your company is greater than 10 percent, increase the ROI target proportionally.

You may be wondering why there are different ROI targets for distributors and manufacturers. This is because manufacturers have greater risks than distributors. Manufacturers may have expensive plants, equipment, and a skilled direct labor force. They have the additional risk of actually making the product. Distributors have the bulk of their assets in inventory and accounts receivable (A/R). These assets are more "liquid"(easier to turn into cash) than those of the manufacturers. Also, distributors can switch from one supplier's products to another supplier's products. In this hypothetical example, various industry publications would be used to determine which marketplaces to survey.

Some of your goals for the new location are to:

- Break-even during the first two years and obtain a 10 percent market share after two years.

- Generate a 10 percent EBIT and 25 percent ROI within the first three years.

- Achieve all of your financial objectives when the new location has a 10 percent market share.

Based on your preliminary research, you determine the following four markets should be investigated further: Denver, Phoenix, San Diego, and San Francisco. The financial analysis of the four cities must be completed before you can make the decision about where the new operation should be located.

Market Research

Next, determine what value-added services the customers want in these marketplaces. This is an important part of the design process because it is crucial to realize that only the customers can determine when a supplier is adding value. You may believe your company has the greatest services, product offerings, and capabilities. But this really doesn't matter until the customers believe it and are willing to pay for those value-added services. The best way to analyze the quality of your services is by asking your customers.

To learn what the customers want, start by discovering what types of customers are in the targeted marketplaces. After becoming knowledgeable about these customers, group them into size categories: small, medium, and large. Also, when your company wants to serve more than one type of customer, be sure the interviews include those customers as well. What is meant by "type" is categories of customers other than size, such as technically advanced, industry leader, growth orientation, and so forth. For this type of information gathering, sampling works well and is also cost-effective. Survey approximately 10 percent of the customers from each of the four market's total available market (TAM). These customers should be randomly selected, unless target customers or target types of customers have been established.

The next step in the design process is to select your survey team. Their task is to write the survey questionnaire. When required, this team should include one or more survey consultants to assist in developing the questionnaire. This is because the wording of the questions is very important to receiving meaningful responses. When preparing survey questionnaires, ask open-ended and closed-ended questions. Open-ended questions cannot be answered with a yes, no, or a specific piece of information, whereas closed-ended questions can. An example of an open-ended question is: What is the biggest problem facing your company today? An example of a closed-ended question is: What are your company's annual sales? Often, the questioner will receive more valuable information by asking open-ended questions, rather than closed-ended questions. (This is because the respondent's answers contain information they believe is important, and it can be information the questioner could not have known to ask. The creative questioner can use this new information to immediately generate new questions and gather even more information. This form of questioning is part of a selling technique known as "funneling." In chapter twenty, funneling is discussed as a powerful selling tool.) The following is an example of a questionnaire for this type of customer survey:

1. What products and services, that are currently unavailable, do your company's customers want? How much would your company's annual sales increase if these additional products and services were available?

2. Does your company plan to expand into new markets? If so, which markets, and over what period of time?

3. What are the biggest problems facing your company today?

4. What are the biggest opportunities available to your company today?

5. What capabilities, products, or services, would you like suppliers to provide?

6. Does your company have a well-balanced inventory? If not, what caused the inventory to be out of balance?

7. What are your company's lead-time requirements, by product and by service?

8. What are the characteristics you value most in a supplier?

9. Where do you envision your company being in terms of size, capabilities, markets, and so forth, in the next two to five years?

10. Do you have any questions that you would like to ask me?

By asking theses types of questions, you can receive valuable information about your company's future customers. Remember, this is a questionnaire based on a hypothetical example. Your actual survey team will write questions specifically tailored to meet your company's requirements. Furthermore, it's a good idea to test the questionnaire on a few customers, rather than conducting the entire survey. This allows your survey team to make changes to the questionnaire when necessary.

Your survey team determines that in order to make a better decision, an *importance factor* is required for each question. This is because some questions are more important than others. Generally, using four numeric values for the importance factor—1, 2, 3, and 4, with 4 representing the most important question—is adequate.

I have found that a good candidate for conducting surveys with customers is a high-ranking manager, preferably the vice president of sales or the sales manager. This person receives firsthand information from the customers. Also, and equally as important, this method provides this person with the opportunity to start developing relationships with new customers.

The manager who conducts the surveys must have excellent "people" skills—especially as a listener. For telephone interviewing, limit the survey time from fifteen to thirty minutes. For face-to-face interviewing, a longer question-and-answer period from thirty minutes to one hour is usually acceptable to most customers. Try keeping the number of questions to a maximum of ten. I've found that customers gladly agree to be interviewed when they know the time requirement and the number of questions.

Set a deadline for completing the customer surveys—preferably one month and no longer than three. When surveys are conducted by a member of a company's management team, conflicts may occur with his or her regular responsibilities. If this occurs, temporarily assign 100 percent of the manager's time to completing the surveys. When this is not practical, retain the services of a professional survey consultant.

Next, schedule the telephone or face-to-face interviews. The completed surveys will generate meaningful information that will help you and your employees design the right distributorship for this marketplace.

Now, review the responses from the surveys immediately after completion. If there is some consistency in the answers, categorize the results by putting them in ranked order, with the largest number of similar responses first. In this hypothetical example, the question-naires contained the following customer's responses:

- 90 percent require a 95 percent fill rate, or better, on standard products
- 80 percent require same-day delivery
- 75 percent believe their inventory is too large in relationship to their sales
- 70 percent said they desperately need technical support for high-end equipment
- 65 percent want to place their purchase orders via e-commerce
- 60 percent said their customers are using new products that their companies are unable to supply

By listing the responses in ranked order, it is easier to understand what products and services are more important to the customers. From a design standpoint, this is very valuable information because the customers have told you what they want and need from a distributor. What more could any potential supplier ask for! The artistry of the design process is using this information to create a profitable new location for your company.

Next, the following question must be answered: What products and services will your new location provide to the customers? As listed previously, the customer surveys have given the answer to this question. Furthermore, the customers said suppliers must provide excellent service and technical support for high-end equipment. Many customers indicated they require a distributor who offers a complete line of entry-level equipment. Now, when customers are interested in purchasing complete systems, they are forced to deal with multiple distributors. Also, this causes them to deal with multiple equipment manufacturers as well. They want an easier and simpler way to have their needs met for these types of equipment requirements.

The customers also said most of the technical employees from the existing distributors require additional training. This forces the customers to contact the equipment manufacturers for answers to complex technical questions. Many customers said they believe manufacturer BEST-PRODUCTS-R-US has an excellent and complete portfolio of entry-level products. By using this information correctly, you can avoid designing another "me-too" distributor. Now, you should learn more about the BEST-PRODUCTS-R-US company.

The BEST-PRODUCTS-R-US company is relatively new in this market. Two of the existing distributors in the four surveyed marketplaces carry their line. Neither distributor is focusing on this manufacturer, as it represents a very small percentage of their sales. Considering this information, you contact the BEST-PRODUCTS-R-US company. During the conversation, they disclose their dissatisfaction with the low sales being generated by their distributors. Furthermore, they are displeased with their entire North American distribution channel. Do you see an opportunity building? Because of this poor performance, they are looking for a distributor who will focus on their line, properly train their sales and technical employees, and make the necessary inventory investment in their products.

At this point in the design process you have several options to consider. Should your new location be a one-stop shop, a value-added reseller (VAR), a limited-line distributor, or a new business model? Because of these various options, it is important to talk with the other manufacturers your company may represent. During these conversations, you discovered most of these manufactures do not require additional distribution in your target marketplaces. But because your company does a great job for them in Los Angeles, the manufacturers agree to work with your company when it involves new business. Also, the manufacturer's technical sales representatives (TSRs) who cover Los Angeles support your target markets as well.

Now, take your first pass at developing a "line card" (product offering). At the top of a columnar-lined pad of paper or software spreadsheet, establish headings for two columns. Call one "Franchised Manufacturers Required," and the other "Non-Franchised Manufacturers Required." Then determine the served available market (SAM) for each marketplace. The SAM is the percentage of the total available market a company serves (sells), based on its line card. For instance, the TAM for personal computer ink jet printers in Chicago is $10 million. When a company can supply 70 percent of the ink jet printer products, the SAM is $7 million ($10,000,000 x 70 % = $7,000,000).

Based on the analysis of the franchised and non-franchised manufacturers your company can represent, the SAM for each of the four marketplaces is 75 percent. The largest of the four markets is San Francisco at $250 million.

Example:

TAM $	$250,000,000
SAM %	x 75 %
SAM $	$187,500,000

Earlier you determined that a 10 percent market share was a reasonable expectation for your company's new location. For your company's industry, a 10 percent market share is the minimum level your new location must achieve to be a factor in the marketplace. With a 75 percent SAM, is it valid to assume your new location will have annual sales of $25 million ($250,000,000 x 10 % = $25,000,000) in a reasonable amount of time? When your new location achieves 80 percent (allowance for possible under-performance) of this goal, will it still meet your financial objectives? More analysis must be done to answer these questions.

Example:

SAM $	$187,500,000
Probability Factor %	80 %
Reasonable SAM $	$150,000,000
Target Market Share %	10 %
Target SAM Sales $	$15,000,000

Whenever you analyze an opportunity that involves a TAM and a SAM, remember to include the SAM portion of the calculation. No one wants to be in the middle of a growth project and unexpectedly discover the SAM is much smaller than the TAM. The difference between the two can cause a venture's failure.

At this point in the design process it is time for a common-sense test that can be easily accomplished by answering the following questions:

1. Can your new location achieve $15 million in annual sales in two years?

2. Is the $15 million in sales, which is a 6 percent market share not the 10 percent you require, enough to be a factor in the marketplace?

3. How does the $15 million in sales impact your EBIT and ROI goals for the new location?

4. Does the expansion project still seem feasible and worthwhile from a risk and reward standpoint?

When the answers to the questions are "no," stop immediately and restart the design process. A flawed design will yield only flawed results. But when the answers to these questions are "yes," you need to ask what is the best way to design the new location so it will meet or exceed all of your objectives. In this hypothetical example, the answers to the common-sense test questions are "yes." However, the "yes" only applies to one of the four marketplaces—San Francisco. The San Francisco marketplace is $250 million and 50 percent larger than the next largest market. Therefore, you decide that San Francisco will be the location of your company's new branch.

In business, decisions must be made as fast as prudently possible. Many companies don't have the time or financial resources to do in-depth research projects. What you are attempting to achieve is a balance between what is required and what is affordable in terms of money and time. The strategic plan should be appropriate for accomplishing the task at hand. This is a perfect example of why most things in business are shades of gray, not black or white. Managers and employees should use their combined talents and experiences to determine the best approach based on the available information, resources, and time. They should listen to their intuitive senses and learn to be comfortable dealing with indicators, not just scientific proof. Their solution may not be perfect (black or white), but it is the best (gray) solution, given all the variables. Additionally, something will be learned from the process itself.

New Market Team and Finalizing the Design

Next, form the new market team. Their job is to complete the design phase of the project. This involves supplying the necessary detailed information to complete this phase of the project. Also, they must establish a "drop-dead" completion date for the design phase. However, their drop-dead date must meet your overall requirements. You and your management team should work with them to establish a mutually acceptable date. It is important to delegate whenever possible, but you have to monitor what you delegate until it is completed. Furthermore, since this project is a major capital expenditure for your company, the CFO should be a member of this team.

For the next portion of the design process, I usually proceed by focusing on the task, then working backward. The task here is planning a logistics system for the new location that will have the lowest total cost of delivering products to the customers.

1. To determine this, the following questions must be answered: Can the new location do factory drop (direct) shipments?

2. Can it do stock transfers from the Los Angeles location?

3. Are common carriers suitable for its shipments?

4. Are company-owned and operated delivery vehicles a cost-effective option?

5. Would a combination of the previously listed methods work?

6. How should the new location's distribution center be designed?

7. Should the DC be your company's, a third party's, or both?

8. Do your customers want some or all of their consumable products inventory stored within their warehouse?

9. Should your company contract with a fulfillment company to provide all or some of these logistics services?

10. What is the very best method of delivering products to your customers that will meet or exceed their expectations?

Your new market team decides there are five operational design options for entering the new marketplace:

A. All sales would be generated via telemarketing and e-commerce, thereby eliminating the requirements for a local sales office with employees. All other functions would be performed by the Los Angeles location's employees.

B. A local sales office staffed with outside, inside, and technical sales employees.

C. The same design as B, with the addition of a demonstration center.

D. A full-service branch; that is, a combination of B and C with the addition of inventory.

E. A full-service division that provides all order fulfillment services to the customers in the new marketplace.

Next, your new market team develops balance sheets and startup expenses for the five options. To develop an accurate pro forma financial statement, establish separate categories for all significant items.

At a minimum, each of these five options should have the following categories:

EXPENSE CATEGORIES	OPTIONS				
	A	B	C	D	E
Balance Sheet Items					
Cash					
Fixed Assets					
Inventory					
Total Balance Sheet Items					
Profit and Loss (P&L) Items					
Payroll Expense					
Outside Sales					
Inside Sales					
Technical					
Purchasing					
Warehouse					
Delivery					
Administration					
Service					
Contract Labor					
Total Payroll Expense					
Operating Expenses					
Rent					
Utilities					
Freight					
Depreciation					
Travel					
Entertainment					
Miscellaneous					
Total Operating Expenses					

EXPENSE CATEGORIES		OPTIONS			
	A	B	C	D	E
Startup Expenses					
Deposits					
Announcements					
Stationery					
Relocation					
Tenant Improvements					
Supplies					
Payroll					
Contract Labor					
Miscellaneous					
Total Startup Expenses					

The total startup costs, or initial investment (the "I" of ROI), is the totals from the "Total Balance Sheet Items," plus the "Total Startup Expenses" columns. The total startup expense is a very important amount because it is your company's investment in the new location before a sale is made. A good manager will have prepared an accurate pro forma financial statement. There are, however, a surprising number of managers who don't prepare statements, or even estimates, for significant investments. They usually learn after many months, or even years, that their investments are generating a surprisingly low ROI. When they're very lucky, the surprise is positive, but all too often the results are negative. An accurate initial investment must be established to correctly measure the subsequent returns.

Next, your new market team establishes net sales, gross profit (GP), operating expenses, and EBIT projections for each of the new location's five options. I've found forecasting for two or three years works best for most situations. But strategic planning has no specific definition for the time requirements of short-term or long-term plans, as it is based on what is appropriate for each unique situation. When the break-even point and your performance goals are projected to be reached after three years, increase the number of years accordingly. These forecasts should have monthly, quarterly, year-to-date, and annual categories for every item. The format should also contain a comparative category, for measuring the current year's results, to the same category's prior years' results.

The following are two years' projections for the five options. These projections are in thousands of dollars:

	YEAR ONE				
	A	B	C	D	E
Net Sales $	500	1,000	1,000	2,000	2,500
GP %	15	17	19	20	20
GP $	75	170	190	400	500
Operating Expenses $	100	300	350	450	700
EBIT $	-25	-130	-160	-50	-200
Average Investment $	250	500	500	1,000	1,250
ROI %	-10	-26	-32	-5	-16

	YEAR TWO				
	A	B	C	D	E
Net Sales $	1,000	2,000	2,000	6,000	7,500
GP %	15	17	19	20	20
GP $	150	340	380	1,200	1,500
Operating Expenses $	125	350	600	800	1400
EBIT $	25	-10	-220	400	100
Average Investment $	500	1,000	1,000	3,000	3,750
ROI %	5	-1.0	-22	13.3	2.7

	TOTALS AFTER TWO YEARS				
	A	B	C	D	E
Net Sales $	1,500	3,000	3,000	8,000	10,000
GP %	15	17	19	20	20
GP $	225	510	570	1,600	2,000
Operating Expenses $	225	650	950	1,250	2,100
EBIT $	0	-140	-380	350	-100
Average Investment $	375	750	750	2,000	2,500
ROI %	0	-18.7	-50.7	17.5	-4.0

After two years of projected results, only option D, the full-service branch, has a positive EBIT. There is no financial advantage to option E, the full-service division. This option would clone many of the non-sales functions the Los Angeles division provides. From the surveys, the new market team learned that many of the customers saw value in distributors' having local inventory. This is because their businesses are really job shops (job shops, or contract manufacturers, make products or provide services to their customers' specifications). Therefore, on any given day, they don't know their actual material requirements. Some of their orders from customers have same-day or next-day delivery requirements. Also, several customers said they experienced major delivery problems from third-party fulfillment and logistics companies. Frequently, additional delivery problems were caused by factory drop shipments and intercompany stock transfers.

From an ROI standpoint, only option D, the full-service branch, provides your company with positive results. The new market team estimates option D will have an average investment of $4 million during the first two years of operation. When estimating the average investment, assumptions must be made as to how much inventory and A/R are required to support the sales projections. Also, your new branch will be in a growth mode. Therefore, it will require an above-average available-for-sale inventory, as a percentage of net sales, to achieve a high service level. For the first two years of operation the pro forma EBIT is $350,000 (minus $50,000 for year one, plus $400,000 for year two). The average annualized EBIT is $175,000. Therefore, the new location's pro forma ROI is 17.5 percent ($350,000 ÷ $2,000,000). The new location's ROI for year two is 13.3 percent (average investment equals $3,000,000, EBIT of $400,000 equals 13.3 percent).

Now, it's time for another common-sense test: Does it make real-world business sense to do this project, especially when the pro forma EBIT and ROI are below your desired amounts? Your new market team reviews everything. The management team reviews everything. You carefully consider the material from a variety of perspectives, and in the end, you all agree that expansion into San Francisco does pass this common-sense test. Despite the fact that the new location won't achieve your desired results in two years, it is still the right long-term decision for the overall success of your company. Sometimes you must look beyond what the numbers indicate is the right decision. I rarely rely solely on the numbers when making decisions. If the numbers gave us all the information we required, then calculators and computers could make all the decisions. I don't believe business works that way. Do you? Now, take your company's design for the new branch and develop the plan.

Plan

The good news about developing business plans is the availability of high-quality software tools to make your job easier. For business planning, I use Jian BizPlan*Builder* (www.jian.com) and Microsoft Office (www.microsoft.com) products. I found both packages to be very useful, user-friendly, and cost-effective. As with the design phase's pro forma financial statement, it is important to have a category for every item that requires planning.

The Project Manager

Your most important task for the planning phase of the project is the selection of the project manager. This position is crucial to the success of the project, so you must select the very best person. This person is someone who will complete the project on time and within budget, and who fits well within your company's culture. He or she should also have a successful background as a manager. The project manager can be an existing employee, provided he or she is fully qualified for this major assignment. Another reason for carefully selecting the project manager, is that this person could become the branch manager of your new location, when the project is completed.

In this hypothetical example, your Los Angeles Division's operations manager, is an excellent candidate for this position. In addition to being a superior manager, he or she thoroughly understands the business. The new project manager could be a general, operations, project, or sales manager who already lives in San Francisco. The big advantage to this approach is this person would already have business relationships with the customers and suppliers in the marketplace. As the project manager, he or she would learn about your company before the branch opens for business. In any case, you select the Los Angeles division's operations manager to be the project manager because this person is the most qualified.

Project Team

Now that you have a project manager, the two of you must select a project team as well. Their role is to prepare and implement the detailed portion of the plan. This team's members must be very good at what they do. The full-service branch will have functions done locally and at the Los Angeles division. Therefore, the project team must include employees from every department within your company. This could be a large group of employees, as the involvement of every department is required to ensure success. The size of the company and the number of functions being performed will dictate the size of the project team. It may be advantageous to retain one or more consultants to provide best practices knowledge for performing certain functions. The key to building a good project team is having all of your company's functional areas represented by highly competent people. This is a case where using second best, or a random selection, won't do.

In business, most things are dependent variables, not independent variables. In other words, things in business are interrelated. Therefore, the initial planning meeting should include all project team members, because the order fulfillment cycle involves every functional area within a company and all functions are interrelated. Other such team responsibilities as assistant leader, recorder, timekeeper, and so forth, should be selected at this initial meeting as well. It is also important for the project manager to initiate brainstorming, and elicit input from each team member at the first meeting. This is a good way to boost morale and encourage everyone to trust that his/her ideas are important and highly valued. It also permits each member to buy-in to, and take ownership of the project. Before this meeting adjourns, the project team should develop and write their Mission Statement (see the definition and example on page 64) or list of objectives they are to accomplish.

The following is an example of how a leader, who elicited input from his employees in an open, creative, and trusting way, improved the resolution of numerous projects: Recently I attended a fundraiser for the City of Hope (COH) Hospital Bone Marrow Transplant (BMT) department. The main speaker for the evening was Stephen J. Forman, MD, director of the COH's BMT department. During his speech he said the funds raised would buy "chalk, not bricks and mortar." He then explained that bricks and mortar were for buildings, and that chalk was for the blackboards where he and his colleagues developed plans to implement new medical procedures. What struck me about his comments and a subsequent one-on-one discussion with another doctor from the COH was that some of the solutions were created eight to twenty years before the corresponding procedures were used to treat patients.

The doctors at the COH are driven to find curative solutions for various types of cancers and other serious illnesses such as AIDS and diabetes. The reason these solutions took so many years to develop are twofold:

1. They were highly complex medical problems.
2. It was impossible to implement the solutions, because the medical equipment and proven process were unavailable. Therefore, the chalkboard is the perpetual conceptual planning medium for the doctors, medical technicians, nurses, and others. It is where they write their thoughts for others to consider, expand on, or question.

One such solution was a collaboration between the doctors and a medical technician who developed a critical piece of the solution that is now saving lives. Without their combined contributions, the solution could have taken years longer to resolve and many lives would not have been saved.

One by one they are finding curative solutions for complex medical problems. In turn, these solutions become protocols for other medical centers around the world. The process works because of its participatory nature, and because it is fostered by the brilliant leadership of Dr. Forman. It takes tremendous dedication, intelligence, participation, and persistence to resolve complex medical problems. This example illustrates why good project managers and project teams are so important to the success of projects.

Master Schedule

The project manager is responsible for creating the project's master schedule. The master schedule is a list of all tasks, employees, departments, decision points, resources, and due dates required to complete a project. In this example, the master schedule is the plan for your company's new branch. To make a master schedule, you can use such software as Microsoft's MS Project. Be sure the software you select can sort the information in any way that may be required.

Next, the project manager publishes the first draft of the master schedule in at least three ways:

1. By due date
2. By department
3. By the individual involved

If the information is sorted in these ways, all team members and department managers can review their own areas of responsibility and see how it relates to the master schedule.

Your project manager schedules the second planning meeting approximately seven calendar days after publication of the master schedule's first draft. This week between meetings will have allowed each team member sufficient time to thoroughly review the entire master schedule. As I wrote earlier, the order fulfillment cycle has numerous interdependent employees and departments working with one another—thus the requirement to review the entire document. The goal for the second meeting is to finalize the plan.

Gap Analysis

In this example, the master schedule's initial draft indicates it will take five months to open your San Francisco branch. Because of overriding business considerations, you know the branch must open in three months. Therefore, since there is a two-month difference, other options must be explored. In this case, exploring other options means doing a Gap Analysis. A Gap Analysis is the process of evaluating the actual progress of a project, as compared to the anticipated progress of a project. For example, you suddenly realize you are eight weeks behind schedule and attempt to find a way to get back on track. In this case, a Gap Analysis is used to find a solution to the problem of what you and your employees must do in order to open the branch in three months, instead of five, as the master schedule indicates.

The project team reconvenes to start the Gap Analysis. This meeting should be relatively brief, as each team member must now meet with his or her employees or co-workers to develop a method to complete the project two months faster. To complete a project in less time usually requires greater resources or the elimination of a portion of the project. But until the team does a Gap Analysis, no one really knows what is necessary to complete the project in three months. It is important to establish a deadline for this analysis and a date for the next meeting. In this example, the team decides that they require three working days to prepare revised estimates for the project.

At the next meeting the revised plans from each team member are reviewed. These revised plans indicate the labor expense will be 10 percent more. The additional labor expense is for overtime pay and temporary labor. The project manager takes this new information and prepares a revised master schedule.

The revised master schedule confirms that the project can be completed in three months with an increased labor expense of 10 percent. This solution, however, raises a new question: Is opening the branch two months sooner worth the additional labor expense? Every aspect of the project's overall importance must be evaluated, comparing total expenses for three months versus five months for completion. Also, this additional expense must be added to the investment, then the projected ROI must be recalculated.

The next step in the planning phase is not scientific in nature. This is because the items that will be evaluated are the intangibles. These are such items as momentum, perceptions of the customers and suppliers, availability of people, and timing. All things considered, you, your company's management team, project manager, and the project team decide it is still important to open the new branch in three months. Now it's time to make your company's plan a reality.

Make

Until this point in the process the involvement of your entire organization has not been required. Now everyone in the organization will be involved in the project in one degree or another.

Mission Statement

For such significant projects as this, it is important for the people involved with the project to create a Mission Statement. A Mission Statement describes in a few sentences just who, what, when, where, and why something is to be accomplished. Here is an example of a Mission Statement your project team might develop:

In three months, on January 2, our company will be opening a new branch in San Francisco. As part of our ongoing commitment to excellence, we plan to exceed the expectations of everyone with whom we are involved. This will be accomplished by a focused sales approach, providing value-added services, and achieving a 95 percent or better service level and an order fulfillment cycle accuracy of 99.7 percent or more. The branch will have net sales of $2 million or more for the first year of operation. The second year will generate a minimum of $6 million in net sales. Break-even is projected to occur during the second year of operation. The new branch will generate a minimum EBIT of 10 percent, an ROI of 25 percent, and a 10 percent market share within the first three years of operation. Furthermore, from its first day in business, the new branch will use best-in-class practices. This new branch is a significant part of our company's overall strategy to achieve long-term controlled profitable growth.

Project Kickoff

Now it's time to have some fun! Have a project kickoff party for your employees. During the event, read the Mission Statement aloud to all your employees. Make sure they thoroughly understand this document. Explain the importance, and the corresponding intense effort, that will undoubtedly occur during the next three months. Display the Mission Statement and master schedule where they can be seen by everyone. Also, such handouts as laminated 3-inch by 5-inch cards or business cards are helpful pocket-sized reminders. Have the Mission Statement printed on one side and the person's business card on the other. Depending on your company's culture, you may want to give the employees T-shirts or coffee mugs that graphically describe the project. Let your employees know there will be monthly meetings to review the master schedule. The key thing to communicate is that this is a team effort and every employee's contribution is important to the success of the project. Again, make it a fun event. People are much more likely to have positive attitudes about the project if it is reinforced by a positive experience.

Selecting the Branch Manager

Considering the January 2 date for opening the San Francisco branch, the project start date is October 1. You select the Los Angeles division's operations manager, who is currently the project manager, as the San Francisco branch manager. This gives you several interesting opportunities to consider. Your company's growth gives all the employees an opportunity for growth as well. This allows you to promote from within, while continuing to groom other employees. Since you are promoting your operations manager, this provides an opportunity for another internal promotion. Obviously, these promotions are based on the required capabilities existing in one of your employees. If these capabilities do not exist in one of your employees, then you have the opportunity to strengthen your organization by hiring someone. When searching for a new operations manager, try to find someone more capable, and with more upside potential than the recently promoted operations manager. Again, you should always be looking for ways to strengthen the organization, thus preparing it for future profitable growth.

In this example, the project manager requires training to become a branch manager. When a company is in an above-average growth mode, it is especially important to lead, train, and motivate all your employees. Many managers make a mistake in believing the leading, training, and motivating they do are only for non-supervisory employees. Nothing could be further from the truth. All employees require your leadership, training, and motivational skills. (This topic was covered in much more detail in chapters one and two.)

Reviewing the Master Schedule

Until your new branch is open for business, the master schedule must be reviewed by the project team on at least a weekly basis. A Gap Analysis must be completed for every task behind schedule. This is to ensure that the new branch opens on time, no matter what! When these meetings are held with less frequency than weekly, too much time might pass and it may become impossible to get the project back on schedule. This is especially true when the project is only three months long, as in this case.

Because your employees have done such a good job in the design and plan phases, the make phase goes extremely well. Since there were only a few Gap Analyses required, the San Francisco branch opens for business as designed and planned on January 2.

Measure

The measure phase of a project determines how the company is performing in relation to the established standards, goals, targets, and budgets. The measurement tools must be in place on the first day any project is started. In this example, at a minimum you would measure all financial targets, product quality, on-time delivery, service level, shipping accuracy, the order fulfillment cycle, and the "Hit Rate." The Hit Rate is the booked customer's orders as a percentage of quoted opportunities. For more meaningful results, measure the Hit Rate in four ways:

1. Products
2. Dollars
3. Request for Quotations (RFQs)
4. Customers

When your company has more than one type of product or service with more than one salesperson or sales territory, you require additional individual categories. This will make the individual results more measurable, and therefore, more meaningful. For example, this is the Hit Rate page or screen layout for January:

Number of Products Quoted	1,000
Number of Products Booked	700
Hit Rate % of Products Quoted	70%
Dollars Quoted	$10,000,000
Dollars Booked	$ 5,000,000
Hit Rate % of Dollars Quoted	50%
Number of RFQs Quoted	200
Number of RFQs Booked	120
Hit Rate % of RFQs Quoted	60%
Number of Customers Quoted	100
Number of Customers Booked	55
Hit Rate % of Customers Quoted	55%

Why is the Hit Rate so important? Booking activity is always important, but it is critical for a new branch or company. Bookings create immediate sales or back orders. You must also know which customers are placing orders and which salespeople are bringing in the RFQs and the orders. Also why does every RFQ not become an order? As you can see from the above example, the Hit Rate percents vary by category. Rarely, if ever, will all the percentage results be the same. When there is more than one category of booking activity, the above summary reporting is required for each category. Also have daily, month-to-date, year-to-date, and prior year-to-date totals for all categories. Since this information is produced to increase bookings and sales, provide these screens or reports to your sales manager and salespeople. This allows them to measure their performance on an ad hoc (as required), rather than on a predetermined frequency.

Many managers, including me, want to know how many verbal RFQs become booked orders during the first telephone call from the customer about their requirement. When the customer's verbal RFQ was not booked during the first call, what were the causes and results of that inquiry? Is it a pending sale or a lost sale? When it is a lost sale, what were the causes? In the case of lost sales, there are at least five categories to measure:

1. The company does not offer the product for sale.
2. An insufficient quantity was available for sale.
3. The lead time was too long.
4. This price was too high.
5. Other causes, with an explanation field large enough for a few sentences.

The lost sales information should be directed to the general manager, sales manager, salespeople, and materials manager on a real-time basis. Then the information should be summarized on a weekly basis. The summarized information allows you and your managers to see what caused your company to lose business: Should you add one or more suppliers to your company's line card? Are your company's lead times too long? Does your company's pricing need to be adjusted? This information allows you and your managers to make informed decisions about products, pricing, and levels of service. (All of this improves your company's Hit Rate and is done to improve your company's controlled profitable growth.)

Today, an ever-increasing percentage of business is done via fax, online order entry, or over the Internet. All of the aforementioned methods of doing business fall under the broadest definition of e-commerce. E-commerce means business done electronically. Therefore, measure e-commerce activity as separate booking and sales categories. This allows you and your sales manager to see the e-commerce results, as it will not be included with other methods of selling.

As with any type of measuring, if the wrong item is selected, or it is measured incorrectly, the results will inevitably be wrong. These erroneous results can lead your company down the wrong path, and it won't be the path to success. The following is an example of how to avoid such a problem: When a company sells a new product in North America, divide the SAM (served available market) into several regional territories. At a minimum there would be the following regional territories: Western USA, Central USA, Eastern USA, Canada, and Mexico. When all five territories are selling $100,000 per month of the new product, are all five territories performing the same? The answer is no. But to know why the answer is no, the following questions must be answered:

1. What is the SAM for each of the five markets?
2. What percentage of each market's SAM does the $100,000 per month in new product sales represent?
3. Which divisions, which salespeople, or methods of e-commerce are generating the sales?

As you can see, if e-commerce is not a separate category and it generated 80 percent of the new product sales in a territory, the wrong conclusion about performance could be made. Also, if the Western USA market is five times larger than Mexico's market, shouldn't its sales of the new product be five times greater? Through this example you can see why it is so important to establish the measurement system correctly. A key to establishing accurate measurement systems is in having individual categories for *who* did the work; *what* were their results; *when* was it done; *where* was it done. When the design, plan, make, and measure phases are completed, the analyze phase is used to determine *why* these are the results.

Analyze

The analyze phase uses the results from the measure phase to determine *why* something is beyond, at, or behind expectations. All elements of the project are examined during this phase. These elements include all financial targets, employees, management, methods, quality, and technology. In other words, it is a super Gap Analysis of every significant aspect of the project.

There are many ways to analyze a project, but I recommend using one of the simpler approaches. A simpler method helps you and your employees avoid "analysis paralysis." Analysis paralysis occurs when you or your employees continue to evaluate a situation, thereby postponing the resolution of the problem. This happens because many people are afraid to make mistakes. As the manager, you should reinforce that learning from our mistakes is a very important part of gaining knowledge and wisdom. Your employees must be taught that implementing a partial solution to a problem, even when it isn't perfect, is absolutely acceptable. This is because when the problem is ongoing, it is negatively impacting your company every day. The longer it takes to resolve the problem, the more money it costs your company.

The following is an example of analysis paralysis: A company has ten salespeople. Two salespeople account for 80 percent of the company's sales and EBIT. The company's sales manager has trained, coached, and prodded the eight low-producing salespeople for six months, with no significant improvement. The sales manager's solution to this problem is to take another six months to interview, and then hire eight new salespeople, one at a time. The rationale behind the sales manager's logic is that it is easier and more cost-effective to train eight salespeople at once, rather than one at a time. I buy that part of the logic. But what about having six more months of low sales from 80 percent of the company's sales force? The obvious and acceptable partial solution is to replace all the low-performing salespeople as fast as possible, even if it is one at a time. And in this example, maybe the sales manager should be replaced as well.

One way to keep this analysis process moving is to focus on the biggest problems first. To do this, rank the results in "worst-first" order. List the worst problems first in terms of dollars and percents. This allows you and your employees to see and resolve the biggest problems first, and not be overwhelmed by trying to fix everything at once. When a partial solution is implemented, it has some immediate positive impact on the results. Fortunately, business is not brain surgery, although it can cause plenty of headaches when improperly managed. A partial solution should be implemented, even when it may take weeks or months to resolve all of your company's problems. This is because business is about making money, with the least amount of investment, in the shortest amount of time. Saving time is one way to make money. The faster a positive change is made, the sooner your company will make more money.

Depending on the item being measured, analyze the results on a daily, monthly, quarterly, or annual basis. When your company is part of a fast-paced industry, or involved in a short-term project, you may require doing this process hourly or on a real-time (actual) basis. Many years ago I helped complete a software conversion project that was improperly designed, planned, implemented, and measured. But it was properly analyzed, and unfortunately easy to do so, because the software conversion was on the verge of putting a division out of business.

Because of the software conversion, the normally well-organized top-performing division was a disaster zone. I used what I call the Crisis Situation Corrective Action Plan process to get things back under control. This process included:

- Sampling such information as sales orders, packing slips, invoices, and purchase orders in an active business environment on an hourly basis.

- Meeting with the general manager and his employees hourly for five to ten minutes to analyze the results of the sampling.

- Developing corrective action plans with a date, employee, and time for each action item.

These hourly meetings continued for two exhausting weeks. Then we went to daily meetings. Finally, after two months of meetings and implemented corrective action plans, the division was stabilized. In this situation, we did what we had to do to keep the division going while we completed the conversion. We did what was necessary and appropriate for that situation. The urgency of the problem forced us to implement partial solutions. If we would have waited until we knew how to resolve every problem, and then implemented them all at once, the division would have gone out of business. When things improved, we changed our methods of operating and proceeded accordingly.

Financial Statements

The ultimate analysis tool for a company is its financial statement. The financial statement is the company's scorecard of results. All financial reporting must be done per generally accepted accounting principles (GAAP). GAAP is a widely accepted set of conventions, procedures, rules, and standards for reporting financial information as established by the Financial Accounting Standards Board (FASB). A financial statement consists of two general categories of information: The first is the balance sheet and the second category is the profit and loss (P&L) statement. The balance sheet has two sections: assets and liabilities. As the words imply, the assets and liabilities must be in balance to be accurate. Therefore, what the company owns (assets) must be in balance with what it owes (liabilities), plus the shareholders' equity, or the net worth of the company.

Assets can be divided into three sub-categories: current assets, fixed assets, and other assets. Current assets are such items as cash, inventory, accounts receivable (A/R) less allowances for bad debts. Fixed assets are such items as land, buildings, machinery, and office equipment—less accumulated depreciation. Other assets are such items as patents and security deposits. Liabilities have two subcategories, current liabilities and long-term liabilities. Current liabilities are such items as accounts payable (A/P), notes payable, accrued (owed) expenses payable, and income tax payable. Long-term liabilities are such items as long-term debt, loans, and mortgages. The shareholders' equity is the company's retained earnings and capital contributions to the company for equity.

Example:

BALANCE SHEET

ASSETS		LIABILITIES	
Current Assets		**Current Liabilities**	
Cash	$ 750,000	A/P	$1,000,000
A/R	1,500,000	Notes Payable	700,000
Less: allowance for		Accrued Expense Payable	200,000
bad debts	<100,000>	Income Tax payable	200,000
Inventories	1,250,000		
Total Current Assets	$3,400,000	Total Current Liabilities	$2,100,000
Fixed Assets		**Long-Term Liabilities**	
Land	500,000	First Mortgage	$1,500,000
Buildings	2,000,000	Total Liabilities	$3,600,000
Machinery	750,000		
Office Equipment	100,000	Shareholders' Equity	
Less: accumulated		Capital Stock	
depreciation	<1,000,000>	Preferred Stock	500,000
Total Fixed Assets	$2,350,000	Common Stock	1,000,000
		Retained Earnings	650,000
		Total Shareholders' Equity	$2,150,000
		Total Liabilities and	
Total Assets	$5,750,000	Shareholders' Equity	$5,750,000

Most managers and owners have several common goals for their companies. They desire earnings before taxes (EBT), and a return on equity (ROE)—equity being the total investment in the business—greater than they could earn from a passive investment (bonds, CDs, insured savings accounts, mutual funds, or stocks). The P&L statement shows how much money the company is making or losing during the year. The following is an example of a P&L for a typical manu-facturing company.

Example:

PROFIT AND LOSS STATEMENT

Categories	Amounts	Percent	Definitions
Gross Sales	$10,100,000	101%	Total sales before discounts and allowances
Less: discounts, returns, allowances	<100,000>	<1%>	Invoice discounts taken by customers and allowances and (uncollected A/R) for bad debts
Net Sales	$10,000,000	100%	Sales after invoice discounts taken by customers and allowances for bad debts have subtracted
Material	$2,000,000	20%	Material used by manufactures in making a product, and purchased by distributors for reselling
Outside Processing	200,000	2%	Services performed by a company's suppliers on company owned materials
Direct Labor	3,000,000	30%	The labor used by manufacturers to make something
Manufacturing Burden	1,500,000	15%	The indirect labor, supplies, and operating expenses used by a manufacturer to make something
Cost of Goods Sold	$6,700,000	67%	The material, outside processing, direct labor, and manufacturing burden total
Gross Profit	$3,300,000	33%	Net sales less the cost of goods sold
Administrative Expense	500,000	5%	Payroll and non-payroll administrative expenses
Sales Expense	500,000	5%	Payroll and non-payroll sales expenses

R&D Expense	200,000	2%	Research and development
Other Expenses	100,000	1%	All miscellaneous expenses
Operating Expenses	$1,200,000	13%	The administrative, sales, and other expenses total
EBIT	$2,200,000	20%	Gross profit less operating expenses
Interest	200,000	2%	Interest paid by the company
EBT	$2,000,000	18%	EBIT less interest
Income Taxes due	600,000	6%	Taxes due the government
Net Profit	$1,400,000	12%	EBT less taxes due the government

For managing your company on a day-to-day basis, it is imperative to always have enough working capital. Working capital is the company's current assets less its current liabilities. The result from this calculation is the current ratio. For example, when a company has $2 million of current assets and $1 million of current liabilities, the current ratio is 2.0 to 1.0. You and your CFO or certified public accountant (CPA) must determine what is the correct ratio for your company. Part of this decision depends on you and the company's collective tolerance for risk. Some of the risk is determined by the amount of operating expenses in relation to the amount of cash in the company. In other words, do you have enough cash to keep your company in business? As the manager, you must determine what is the right balance of risk and reward for your company.

You may have noticed more of this chapter is devoted to the design phase than the other phases. This was done by design (pun intended). An excellent design will make every feature of your operation easier, more economical, and faster.

Summary

The artistry of managing the Design, Plan, Make, Measure, and Analyze Process lies in using these procedures regularly as tools to achieve controlled profitable growth. Mastering this process can yield the results you desire for any project or company. This process requires all of your management skills, for it entails every aspect of growing a company. Your commitment and perseverance in using this process are critical. It can help you to achieve the desired results for your company with the least amount of time and money.

Cash Is King and the Golden Rule

CHAPTER EIGHT

Money is the root of many good things. Money is used to build hospitals and hire doctors, nurses, and technicians who care for injured and sick people. It is also used to build schools, pay for education, and to house and feed the less fortunate. Tax revenues are used to protect our citizens and country. Having money to spend is made possible by good employees, investors, managers, and business owners doing great work. This creates opportunities for all of us in the process. Earning money and using it wisely are good things.

Managers and their companies are in business to serve customers, employees, shareholders, suppliers, and the community. It takes good employees and sufficient capital for good managers to build a business properly. Money is the fuel of business. Used wisely, it funds profitable growth, creates jobs, provides excellent goods and services, and generates above-average returns for the investors.

I earned my first return on investment (ROI) at the age of five. It happened when my kindergarten class was taken to a local bank by our teacher for the purpose of opening a savings account. Each student, including my lifelong friend, Neil Berlant (whom I mentioned in the acknowledgments section of this book), had at least five dollars for opening his or her account. After opening our accounts, we were given bank passbooks with our initial deposits posted. We were also given a small tin can with a coin slot we could save money at home, between bank visits.

One month later we returned to the bank with our passbooks and the money we saved. I handed the bank teller my money and my passbook. She processed my deposit and returned my passbook with the new transaction recorded. I can still remember looking inside my passbook and seeing a word and corresponding number that seemed magical to me. My original balance had become larger because of an entry called "interest." I asked my teacher what "interest" meant, and she explained it to us.

From that day onward, I have saved and invested money. I quickly realized that money would give me the power and freedom to purchase what I wanted. I also learned at an early age that my financial wealth would increase according to how much I saved and then wisely invested. My kindergarten experience taught me the importance of having cash to invest and seeing a return on investment. (My friend Neil is a successful investment banker and stockbroker today so kindergarten was a stellar year for him as well.)

As you may have heard many times before, the term "golden rule" in business means "whoever has the gold, rules." Business is about money and generating good returns. In business, money equals power, hence another often used saying: "Cash is King." Despite the fact that one sees positive results, business investing is not about earning interest, unless being a lender or banker is your business. Business is about taking risks (investing) to generate rewards (returns). These rewards are potentially greater than those you could earn from safe and passive investments such as certificates of deposit (CDs), government bonds, and insured savings accounts.

Sources of Cash

Before doing anything in business, determine how much cash you can invest and risk. When you are starting a business, the cash can come from you, family members, partners, high net worth individuals, government programs, and venture capital firms. For privately held companies that are ongoing businesses, cash can also come from banks and other lending institutions. Publicly held companies can receive cash from the issuance and sale of common stock, preferred stock, and debentures. Also, for all forms of ongoing businesses, cash is generated from the sale of such assets as equipment, inventory, and real estate.

Pro Forma and Cash Flow Statements

To determine how much cash your company requires, prepare a Pro Forma Financial Statement and Cash Flow Analysis Statement.

A Pro Forma Financial Statement is a projection, based on prudent estimates, as to how a company will perform in the future. The Cash Flow Analysis Statement shows how much cash a company requires to achieve those projections. Pre tax cash flow in business is stated as earnings before interest taxes depreciation and amortization (EBITDA).

Fundamental Financial Terms

Other significant financial terms used in the pro forma financial and cash flow analysis statements include: accounts payable (A/P), accounts receivable (A/R), capital expenditures (Cap-X), cost of goods sold (COGS), gross profit (GP), inventory, net sales, operating expenses, operating income or earnings before interest and taxes (EBIT), and earnings before taxes (EBT).

- Accounts payable is the money owed by the company to its suppliers.
- Accounts receivable is the money owed to a company by its customers.
- Capital expenditures are investments in depreciable fixed assets.
- Gross profit is a company's net sales minus its cost of goods sold.
- Operating expenses, or overhead, are the expenses required to run a company.
- Inventory is an asset purchased for manufacturing, modifying, or reselling in the operation of a company.
- Net sales are a company's total sales minus certain returns, allowances, and discounts.
- The terms EBIT and EBT are self-explanatory.

Today, there are many software tools (see chapter seven) available to help you prepare these projections. However, before using any projections to get a line of credit for your company, have it reviewed by a CPA. These projections are the cornerstones of the managers' business plans for their companies. Therefore, they must be accurate.

Examples

When a company grows rapidly, it requires additional cash to support the growth. But when a company is in a recession and remains profitable, generally it will "throw off" cash. The following are examples of growth, no growth, and recession scenarios for a $12 million company:

	Growth	No Growth	Recession
Net Sales at 100%	$18,000,000	$12,000,000	$6,000,000
COGS at 70%	12,600,000	8,400,000	4,200,000
GP at 30%	5,400,000	3,600,000	1,800,000
Operating Expenses at 20%	3,600,000	2,400,000	1,200,000
EBITDA at 10%	1,800,000	1,200,000	600,000
Inventory at 45 Days of Sales	2,250,000	1,500,000	750,000
A/R at 45 Days of Sales	2,250,000	1,500,000	750,000
Cash required to support $750,000 of A/R and $750,000 of Inventory Growth	$1,500,000	$ 0	($1,500,000)

As you can see, an additional $1,500,000 ($2,250,000 plus $2,250,000 equals $4,500,000 minus $3,000,000 equals $1,500,000) of cash is required to support the growth scenario. This is derived from the required increases of $750,000 each in A/R and inventory. Also, the additional cash from EBITDA is only $600,000 ($1,800,000 minus $1,200,000 equals $600,000), thus forcing an additional infusion of cash, such as borrowing, to satisfy this cash requirement. Conversely, there is excess cash of $900,000 ($3,000,000 minus $1,500,000 equals $1,500,000 minus $600,000 of lower EBITDA equals $900,000) in the recession scenario. Also, it is important to note that we are only looking at the cash requirements related to inventory and A/R. Software tools and your CFO or CPA can provide you with more sophisticated cash flow analyses. The main point of this example is that sales growth usually requires cash in addition to the EBITDA of a company.

Determining the Cost and Risk of Capital

Generally, the greater the risk of capital as determined by the lender, the more expensive the cost of cash will be to the company. The cost of cash to the company is in direct relation to the company's financial strength. Usually, asset-based borrowing from banks and mortgage lenders are the least expensive methods of getting cash for a company. The interest rates these institutions charge are usually based on the prime rate or the London Inter Bank Offered Rate

(LIBOR). The prime rate is the lowest rate of interest commercial banks charge large, credit-worthy companies. LIBOR is the rate at which banks and mortgage lenders can borrow from wholesale money markets. All other costs of borrowing vary tremendously, depending on the lending rates and the negotiating skills of the lender and borrower.

Bankers and Investment Bankers

Having a good relationship with your banker is essential to the long-term success of your company. It can facilitate future negotiations with favorable terms and conditions for your company. Unless you are a CPA or very financially astute, your company's CFO or CPA should be involved with all bank negotiations. Bankers and CPAs share a common vocabulary. They use such terms as "point," which means 1 percent, and "sub-debt," which is a debt that is subordinate (less secure) to other debt. The term "revolver" means a revolving line of credit, and "senior debt" means the most secure form of debt, such as preferred stock and bank debt. As you can see from these few examples, the world of finance has a unique language. The last thing you want is to find yourself in a situation involving money and be at a disadvantage because you aren't familiar with the terminology. My glossary includes most of the basic words used in finance, but it might be a good idea to invest in a business/finance dictionary. I frequently use the Web glossaries of such business-related companies as Charles Schwab (www.schwab.com), Money World (www.moneyworld.com), Morningstar (www.morningstar.com), and Quicken (www.quicken.com).

Sometimes, it's best to retain an investment banker for decisions regarding significant amounts of cash. The main functions of investment bankers are to underwrite new investment securities and to represent a person, group, or company for the purpose of consummating a transaction. Their key role is to negotiate the most favorable terms for a client. Investment bankers' compensation is usually in the form of a success fee, which means they receive their fee when the transaction is consummated. During strong economic cycles, when the demands for investment banker services are high, they may charge a retainer fee to cover their initial administrative expenses.

There is no standard fee for investment bankers. Therefore, the fee agreement is based on the negotiating skills of the people involved. It is important to note that good investment bankers are supreme negotiators. It is part of what they do to earn their fees. I once had to negotiate with a highly skilled investment banker to structure his fee agreement. He had much more experience and skill in negotiating than I, so I sought the counsel of my very talented business attorney, Mark Lindon, to negotiate for me, thus "leveling the playing field." The final agreement was a win-win for the investment banker and me.

Loan Agreements

After determining your company's cash requirements, and how the debt is going to be supported, negotiate and consummate a loan agreement. The cash companies receive from their lenders can be used for various business purposes, as long as they are within the covenants (guidelines) of the loan agreement. These covenants include various terms, conditions, and financial ratios the company's management must maintain. If these terms are violated, the company may face costly penalties, and it might have to immediately repay the loan's balance.

Summary

The artistry of managing cash is always knowing your company's cash position and having sufficient cash and lines of credit to support your company's current and future requirements. Cash is a company's fuel. Once you know your company's cash position, you and your managers must make prudent business decisions to maximize the company's ROE. Whether your company is a startup or an ongoing business, it is impossible to properly implement any significant business plans until you know how much cash is available. It is best to know the company's cash position on a real-time basis. However, if this is not possible, you should know the company's cash position at least daily. On a monthly basis, you should know your company's future projected cash requirements for a minimum of twelve months. These cash requirement projections should be in weekly and monthly categories. The current and future cash requirements must be clearly highlighted in relation to the terms, conditions, and financial ratios of the company's loan agreement. This is an area of managing a company in which you definitely don't want any surprises.

The Business Cycle, Customer Satisfaction, and Service

A business cycle without customer satisfaction is only a series of transactions, from start to finish. Customer satisfaction adds value to the business cycle. It can be the difference between the success or failure of companies with identical business cycles.

A successful business cycle that provides customer satisfaction for existing distributors and product line manufacturers begins when a company has the right employees and the right inventory in sufficient quantities available for sale. For contract manufacturers, the business cycle that provides customer satisfaction becomes successful when the company has the ability to meet or exceed the customer's requirements for making parts, sub-assemblies, or assemblies. The company's capabilities may be internal or attained through outsourcing. For all businesses, the cycle ends when the customer's payment for products delivered and services rendered are cleared by the company's bank.

Excellent customer service is ultimately defined and determined by customers, but it begins when a company meets or exceeds the customers expectations. High-quality customer service requires excellent distribution and manufacturing management. To determine the quality of a company's customer service, there are four categories to measure and report. These four quality attributes apply to most businesses:

1. Product quality. One hundred percent product quality is achieved when the parts received by the customers meet their specifications.

2. On-time delivery: One hundred percent on-time accuracy is attained when the parts ordered by the customer arrive at their dock, on the required due date, and in some cases, at the required time of day.

3. Service level (fill rate): One hundred percent service level is accomplished when a customer's product requirement for a standard product is filled completely.

4. Shipping accuracy: One hundred percent shipping accuracy occurs when a company fills a customer's purchase order precisely.

Customers want and expect suppliers to provide excellent product quality and on-time delivery, to maintain an excellent service level, and to pride themselves on consistent shipping accuracy. The service levels are measured on standard products only. Standard products are those products a company or its suppliers list as "regular stocking items" in their price books and other literature. Therefore, these parts are not "specials." For example, how often would you shop at a grocery store that was constantly out of such standard products as eggs, milk, bread, and paper towels? Our customers look at our businesses in the same way.

There are several ways to measure product quality, on-time delivery, service level, and shipping accuracy. I've used the following calculation for several decades to measure these functions. This method for measurement consistently met or exceeded the customer's expectations: A score of 1 is earned when the activity being performed, or the product that was manufactured, was done correctly. When the activities were not done correctly, or the product was manufactured incorrectly, a score of 0 is earned. The following calculation is used to measure all four categories of quality:

Example:

Number of Product Transactions	=	1000
Activity or Product Accuracy	=	995
Quality Level %	=	99.5%

Every company's management establishes what is and what is not the acceptable standard for product quality, on-time accuracy, and shipping accuracy. Generally, and as of this writing, I've found that most aerospace, non-high-tech, and non-medical industrial companies have 99.7 percent accuracy as an acceptable level of quality. This standard allows for 3 errors per 1,000 units or transactions. I have also found that most aerospace, high-tech, and medical companies use six-sigma quality as their standard. Six-sigma quality allows a maximum of 3.4 errors per 1,000,000 units or transactions. The term "six sigma" is generally used to indicate that a process is under control, meaning it is plus or minus three sigma from the center line of a "control chart." A control chart has upper and lower limits where values of some statistical measures for a series of parts are plotted. Frequently it will have a center line to help indicate a trend of the plotted values toward either control limit.

Through hundreds of conversations with customers, suppliers, and salespeople, I've learned that when distributor or product line manufacturers have service levels above 95 percent, they are usually able to meet or exceed their customer's requirements. Some people believe companies cannot afford to have service levels greater than 95 percent. From firsthand experience, I know this is not the case. I was responsible for a $150 million business group that achieved a service level of 95 percent or better for five consecutive years. The sales and EBIT improved dramatically, increasing by approximately 300 and 400 percent, respectively, over the same five-year period. (As an aside, this business group performed so well that the parent company sold it for approximately $41 million in 1998. This business group was valued at $10 million in 1993. The 95 percent plus service level was one of the key factors in achieving the excellent performance results and thus added to the high improvement in shareholders' value.)

Companies can achieve and benefit from having high service levels. This can be seen in the example given in the previous paragraph, in which a company had the right employees and the right inventory management system. The employees' proficiency included managing the inventory with the lowest total cost per transaction. Also, the buyers, purchasing agents, and material managers were taught how to maximize the "terms and conditions" offered by the suppliers. They knew how to enhance the overall GP and the GP per transaction for the material they managed.

Summary

Having too much inventory will not necessarily generate a high service level. For example, if a company is selling ten units per month of a product and that product has a one-week lead time, is there any value in having a hundred units available for sale? Obviously, the answer is "no." Then why do so many companies have so much excess inventory? Usually, managers try to justify the excess inventory by saying, "It's not really excess inventory. It's all good-moving product." It may be "good-moving product," but taking the "more is better" approach to inventory management is not a good idea. This approach only increases the company's investment, without improving its service level. The artistry of managing the business cycle lies in having the lowest total cost per transaction, while providing the maximum level of customer satisfaction. Providing excellent customer service requires you and your employees to have a proactive mind-set. This is because a company must have the necessary employees, infrastructure, inventory, management, quality standards, and services in place to provide high levels of customer satisfaction. Every employee must be trained and friendly, demonstrating that "the customer is our business." Business must be done in such a way that every customer is satisfied. This is a constant re-educating challenge in today's downsized companies where being reactive may be the norm. As the manager, you must know that all of your employees treat every customer in a positive, proactive way. The business cycle is perpetual. Continuous improvement for customer satisfaction should be a goal for every company.

Computer Consultants, Software, and Hardware

Warning: Reading this chapter can cause extreme drowsiness. Therefore, if you are not shopping for a new computer system or wanting to gain general computer system knowledge, proceed to chapter eleven.

When this book is published, the software, hardware, or services recommendations I've made may have changed. This is because of the steady stream of new products or enhancements to existing products. But the process for selecting a computer system is likely to remain the same for some time.

The need to upgrade is one of the major problems that comes with selecting a computer system (software, hardware, networks, services, etc.) for any company. Also, this is one of the main reasons so many managers have made major mistakes in this area. Many of us feel somewhat insecure about this topic. It is highly technical and complex. Many of us know the buzz words and just enough technical information to get by. Therefore, we are dependent on technical employees or consultants to help us make the right decision. There are, however, some general requirements you should follow when selecting a computer system.

Required Documentation

When beginning a search for new application software (software), there are two mission critical documents required:

85

1. A complete documentation package that defines the current system's functionality.
2. A complete specification package as to how you and your employees want the company's future system to operate.

If you and your employees have never gone through this process, it may become a very lengthy task as it can take hundreds of hours to complete the documentation and specification packages listed. This takes a lot of hard work, knowledge, and experience to do correctly. To gather the required information involves interviewing your company's customers, employees, and suppliers. These discussions should cover current needs, as well as requirements for the next three to five years. If your company doesn't have internal resources to accomplish this task, consider retaining the services of a computer consultant.

Computer Consultants

Good computer consultants are hard to find. When researching computer consultants, select a person or company who doesn't sell any computer system products. By taking this approach you will avoid potential conflicts of interest. It can be difficult for the consultant to furnish you with objective information if there is a vested interest in selling other products and services.

Always conduct a thorough reference check on the consultant. Be sure you talk with the clients who are using a computer system the consultant recommended. Make sure this system has been in an active environment for at least six months. When they have used their system for less than six months, it may be difficult to get an accurate picture about the quality of the consultant's recommendation. Also, find out how many years the consultant has done the specific work your company requires. Is the potential consultant located in close proximity to where you require his or her services? If not, the actual costs may be much greater due to the additional expenses that will be incurred for lodging, meals, and travel. When the consultant has not worked in your company's specific industry, you and your staff may spend a lot of time and expense making the consultant knowledgeable about your industry.

If you manage a large company with multiple locations, you will probably require the services a large consulting firm. Such companies as the Big 5 accounting firms of Arthur Andersen (www. arthurandersen.com), Deloitte & Touche (www.dttus.com), Ernst & Young (www.ey.com), KPMG Peat Marwick (www. kpmgconsulting.com), and PricewaterhouseCoopers (www.pwcglobal. com) offer computer system consulting services. Because these companies are large and well-known, however, doesn't mean you can skip doing your research on them. These companies have good, average, and weak employees just like the companies that may retain their services. Be sure to interview the potential project manager and project team that will be assigned to your company's project. Also, and most importantly, you need the ability to keep or replace any consultant. Without this contractual understanding, you can end up having your project done by the weaker consultants, as the better consultants may be pulled away to work on other contracts.

When possible, instruct the consultant to give your company a fixed-fee or a not-to-exceed proposal. The consultant may not be able to quote this way because he or she doesn't know the scope of the project. When this is the response, ask how much additional interviewing time is required to furnish a fixed-fee or not-to-exceed proposal. Most good computer consultants, who have had experience with your company's type of project, can do this additional interviewing in a reasonable amount of time. They should develop a list of specific job functions that require additional interviewing. The list should include employees and supervisors from every department. This is to ensure that the second round of interviewing determines the requirements for all your company's users. The consultant should not charge for this additional interviewing time, as it is part of their sales expense included in the consultant's fee, provided you retain his or her services.

If you have talented information technology (IT) employees, don't treat them like second-class citizens because you are going to retain consultants. This can do tremendous damage to the morale of the entire department. It is important to remember the term "consultant" doesn't mean "expert." You may find that the consultants are actually less talented and knowledgeable that your own employees. But you still need them on a temporary basis for such large computer projects as conversions. It is the team—employees and consultants—who will do the work, and their positive morale is critical.

Software

When your company is a member of an industry association, determine if there is a list of recommended computer system suppliers. Ask your customers, employees, and suppliers. I've found this is one of the best ways to gather valuable recommendations. Ascertain what the potential computer system providers charge for their various ongoing maintenance services. These annual maintenance fees usually cost between 10 and 15 percent of the initial software expense for standard distribution and manufacturing software packages. Also, for non-maintenance support, will the software provider be available to help with ongoing special support issues? If so, at what cost? Don't be afraid to copy a successful competitor: When another company is using a great computer system, be wise enough to follow its lead and build on its success.

Minimum Functionality Requirements

The following represents the minimum capabilities a computer system should have to be a cost-effective tool for distribution, contract manufacturing, and manufacturing companies:

1. Can the new computer system reduce transaction processing labor and time? Will this cost reduction allow the company to have the lowest total cost of information processing as measured against the best-in-class (companies that are the very best, as compared to the peers) companies? Will the system's cost savings and enhancements generate additional EBIT that will meet or exceed the company's ROI requirements?

2. Can the software, without modification, do 80 percent of the company's specified essential requirements? For the remaining 20 percent or less, does the software provide a fast and cost-effective way to make modifications? When the canned (basic) software is modified, how are new software releases integrated?

3. Does the software have fully integrated and powerful applications for the entire order fulfillment process?

4. Does the system support e-commerce?

5. Are there tools for the employees and managers to measure the productivity of all functions within the company?

6. Will the inventory management module provide customers with a minimum service level of 95 percent? Can this be accomplished while achieving the company's required ROI and return on inventory investment (ROII)? ROII measures the amount of GP dollars generated in relation to the average inventory investment. This is usually calculated monthly, and expressed on an annualized basis. For most non-seasonal businesses, use the prior three month's activities to calculate ROII.

	INVENTORY	GROSS PROFIT
January	$1,000,000	$150,000
February	$1,250,000	$175,000
March	$1,350,000	$175,000
Totals	$3,600,000	$500,000
Average	$1,200,000	$166,666
Calculation	$ 166,000	13.8% Monthly ROII
	$1,200,000 =	x 12 (Annualized)
		165.6% ROII

7. Will the inventory management module automatically generate purchase orders for items that meet the system's criteria for reordering? Can the buyers build purchase orders electronically, and then review them before transmittal to the suppliers?

8. Will the non-system (non-stocking items) purchased products go automatically to the buyers for review?

9. Will the system automatically create a requirement for consumable products that are used with another product? For example, you have a requirement for ten ink jet printers. Will the system automatically create a requisition for ten black and ten color ink jet cartridges?

10. When the company has multiple locations with centralized purchasing, will the system consolidate requirements from all locations into one requisition for each product?

11. When desired, can the buyers review the requirements on a product basis?

12. Is the system capable of providing shipping instructions to the suppliers for multiple company locations? Also, will the sys-

tem provide the suppliers with drop-ship instructions when the product must be delivered to a non-company location—a customer's warehouse, for example?

13. Is the system's item master field large enough for suppliers' part numbers and the company's internal part numbers?

14. Can usage history be transferred from one part number to another? If so, how much history? Depending on the company's requirements, it should be capable of transferring between one to three years of history.

15. How much time does it take to add a new product to the item master?

16. Can purchase orders be printed, auto-faxed, sent via electronic data interchange (EDI), or e-mailed to suppliers?

17. Can the system do branch stock (inventory) transfers?

18. Are there system tools to prevent excess inventory?

19. Is there a control tool for reporting purchase orders transmitted to suppliers that are greater than the system's recommendations?

20. Can the system process "hot buys" (urgent material that must be purchased immediately)? The buyer must be able to see the purchasing requirement immediately after order entry is completed.

21. Can the system recommend products that should be returned to the suppliers? These returns may be caused by supplier's requests, date sensitivity, excess inventory, or other conditions.

22. How does the system calculate the supplier's lead time? Does it use the supplier's actual average lead time, current lead time, or another method?

23. For manufactures and distributors performing value-added (adding labor or outside processing to material) work, can the system manage multiple level (sub-assemblies that are part of an assembly) bills of materials?

24. Is there a back order scheduling tool for loading the manufacturing (supplies, equipment, labor, material, outside processing, and tooling) environment?

25. Can the system receive customers' computer-aided design (CAD), computer-aided manufacturing (CAM), enterprise re-

sources planning (ERP), material requirements planning (MRP), and manufacturing resources planning (MRPII) files?

26. Can the system do "what if" analyses? For example, if a part, sub-assembly, or assembly is given the highest scheduling priority, can the system calculate revised lead times? This revised lead time for the part, sub-assembly, or assembly priority determines what schedule changes will be made to the other parts.

27. Does it have an outside processing module with adequate field sizes for processing instructions, revision levels, and manufacturing drawings?

28. Does the system have an expediting tool for reviewing past-due items and items due within selected date ranges?

29. Will its master schedule accurately project monthly sales?

30. Does the system have a comprehensive customer master? The customer master should have fields for every piece of information about the customers. The customer master requires such fields as customer name, customer number, standard industrial classification (SIC) code, assigned outside salesperson and inside salesperson, and so forth?

31. Does the system have a powerful credit and collection module?

32. Will it allow for entering a customer's order (quote and complete order entry) during the customer's first telephone call? All customer inquiries do not require this type of response. But when there is a time-sensitive requirement, the system must be able to meet the customer's needs.

33. Does the system have remote access capabilities for customers, employees, and suppliers?

34. Does it have networking capabilities?

35. Does it provide management tools for ranking customers by sales, GP percent, and GP dollars per transaction?

36. Can the system track products ordered in relation to products quoted (see Hit Rate on pages 66-67 and 184)?

37. Can the system track lost sales and the reasons why the sales were lost?

38. Will the system provide all employees with the reporting tools to allow for the company's continuous improvement? Can it

provide this information in summary and ad hoc (as required) formats using such tools as a report writer?

39. Is the system capable of ranking information in any format the user wants?

40. Does it provide review information on a real-time, daily, weekly, month-to-date, monthly, year-to-date, annual, and prior-period basis? Can the summary information be displayed on a single screen or printed on one page?

I recently was a member of a North American Graphic Arts Suppliers Association (NAGASA) team that developed a booklet of guidelines on how to select a computer system. The team was made up of graphic imaging industry end-users and a computer consultant. The booklet, entitled *A Guide to Selecting a New Computer System*, is a very useful tool for choosing a computer system. To receive information about this computer guide, contact the NAGASA office at 202.328.8441 or e-mail nagasa@smart.net. You can visit their Web site at www.nagasa.org.

Hardware

For the selection of computer hardware, choose a proven platform that is expandable, easy to operate, and compatible with the software package. It should also have an "open" (easy to connect to other systems) architectural design, and a low maintenance cost. Since open platform computers are relatively new, there is limited system support software available. Soon, this will not be a problem, as more system software tools are constantly being developed for these machines. When your company has technically qualified IT employees, or outside service, operating an open system machine is very manageable. When interviewing the users of the potential software, ask them what type of hardware their companies have, and the annual cost of hardware maintenance. Also, what type of hardware do the software providers recommend? Will they furnish a performance guarantee if your company uses their hardware recommendation? Because of the complexity involved in deciding which hardware to use, this is another area where a good consultant can prove to be invaluable.

Computer System Due Diligence

Never purchase software based solely on a demonstration. Demos are designed to make the software look good. The important thing is the computer system's "actual" results, not the "projected" results. This is another reason why it is beneficial to talk directly with actual users of any system. Find out what their "actual" results are in terms of service level, ROII, credit, collection, inventory, inside sales, distribution center, logistics, customer service, system response time, and total system ownership cost. Also, find out if the user company's inside and outside sales teams believe the new system has improved the order fulfillment cycle and customer service. Usually, they have good information about how the customers are being serviced.

Throughout this book I share with you some of the most important information I've learned about business. Sometimes this may be about products and services. However, what I recommend will always be from either firsthand experience or research. Therefore, if I haven't used or researched it, it won't be recommended in this book. To recommend any specific hardware or software would be contrary to the main point of the chapter—there is no single simple computer system solution that is right for every company. You and your employees must make the investment in time and money to properly do the selection process. I am unaware of any shortcuts to this important and complex task. To get the best system for your company requires the highest levels of preparation, research and due diligence by you and your best employees.

Definition of a Good Computer System

Good computer systems are key to the success of any company. Because of companies' growth requirements, computer systems must be easily expandable. My criteria for what constitutes a good computer system are as follows:

- The system provides the lowest total cost of information processing.

- It is easily expandable and has an open system design.

- The computer system is manufactured and supported by a well-established, financially strong company that has at least five hundred active customers.

- The fully expanded system can support an appropriate number of active users to meet your company's growth plans for preferably ten, but no less than five years, with an average response time of two seconds for all inquiries.

- The company's total cost of information processing is between 0.1 percent and 0.5 percent of net sales. I've found this to be a realistic guideline for most industrial distributors and manufacturers with annual sales between $5 and $500 million.

Computer system conversions usually cause tremendous infrastructure changes. Prepare and train your employees about the ways these potentially dramatic changes may impact how they do their jobs. One measure of a good computer system conversion is when it has been accomplished almost invisibly from a service perspective to your customers and suppliers. Use the Design, Plan, Make, Measure, and Analyze Process that I discussed in chapter seven to help you and your employees achieve successful results.

The financial rewards in business are the EBT and ROE (or ROI). EBT is the difference between your company's costs and selling prices. To accurately evaluate the risk portion of operating a company, you must know your costs, which is the topic of the following chapter.

Summary

The artistry of managing the selection process for a computer system is in choosing one that has the lowest total cost of information processing, meets your essential requirements, meets your present and future requirements, and expands easily to meet upcoming needs. Fortunately, hardware, software, and networks will improve and become less expensive in the process. Selecting the right computer system is one of the most difficult and complex challenges for most managers. It is very important to remember that the computer system can't and won't fix your company's problems. The computer system is a powerful tool for managers and employees. When used properly, it will improve processes while reducing costs and enhancing customer satisfaction.

Know
Your Costs

All costs are variable, not fixed. Most of my associates and friends in the accounting profession disagree with my belief that all costs are variable. Many of them were taught that fixed costs are expenses you have no control over during the day-to-day operating of a company. These are such items as rent, amortization, and deprecation amounts, and so forth. The variable costs include payroll, material, petty cash disbursements, COD payments, supplies, and other expenses. After listening to their arguments against my position, I ask them one question: "Can you name every cost in a company that cannot be increased or decreased?" They usually hesitate while contemplating their answer, and then reply with "Yes, but...." Then, I give them several examples of companies such as Apple Computer, General Electric, General Motors, and IBM in which the CEO made major reorganizations and, in so doing, changed most of the costs. In this process they sold or sub-leased property, plant, and equipment. They also got rid of product lines and entire businesses. When the financial impact was significant, their companies may have taken a special reorganization accounting charge. Everything in life is subject to change, including a company's "fixed" costs.

The determination of whether costs are fixed or variable really isn't the issue, as they are still costs. What is important is having accurate cost information throughout your company's various information systems. It is also important to understand that as the manager, you have the power to change every cost. You must know your company's costs to establish an accurate selling price for any product or service. If you manage a contract manufacturer, you must know the company's costs to prepare an accurate estimate in response to the customer's RFQs. For all types of businesses, this ensures that the company makes the necessary EBIT.

Distributors and manufactures have most costs in common, except for direct labor, research and development, and operating expenses. Some common cost elements are material, outside processing, sales, administration, and other expenses. Manufacturers have the additional expense category of manufacturing burden. This is also referred to as manufacturing overhead. Manufacturing burden expenses are a distributor's operating expenses and depreciation, plus the indirect labor used in the manufacturing process. Indirect labor expense is inclusive of positions as engineers, production controllers, plant managers, operations managers, and maintenance employees. Sometimes when manufacturers have material intensive products, a manufacturing burden is applied to the material as well as to the direct labor. Therefore, this burden goes into COGS.

To accurately prepare a cost estimate, all categories must have their costs properly allocated. The following estimate summary and EBIT summary pro forma for the estimated parts are examples of cost estimates used by manufacturers and distributors:

	Manufacturer	*Distributor*
Material	$1.00	$1.00
Outside Processing	0.50	0.50
Direct Labor	1.00	N/A
Manufacturing Burden	1.00	N/A
Cost of Goods Sold (COGS)	$3.50	$1.50
Selling Price	$5.00	$2.14
(COGS at 70% and GP at 30%)		
Less: Sales Expense at 10%	0.50	0.21
Administration at 5%	0.25	0.11
Cost of Goods Sold	3.50	1.50
Operating Expenses at 5%	0.25	0.11
Estimated EBIT $	$0.50	$0.21
Estimated EBIT %	10%	10%

This example illustrates why it's somewhat easier to prepare an estimate summary for distributors than for manufacturers. Distributors have just two steps to prepare a selling price:

1. Add the material and outside processing costs.
2. Calculate the desired GP.

Manufacturers have the additional cost elements of direct labor and manufacturing burden, that are added to the calculation. The direct labor and manufacturing burden costs are not fixed amounts. Therefore, periodic recalculating is required. Also, the manufacturing burden expense is included in the COGS. The value of manufacturer's inventory usually includes direct labor, material, outside processing, and manufacturing burden required to make the products. Since distributors don't make products, their operating expenses cannot increase the value of their inventory. Distributors' and manufacturers' inventory is usually valued in one of three ways: first-in-first-out (FIFO) basis, a last-in-first-out (LIFO) basis, or average unit cost method.

For manufacturers, a detailed estimate is required before an estimate summary can be completed. This involves breaking down the total direct labor hours required to manufacture a part into separate operations. An operation describes how a specific function is performed, how much time is required to manufacture one piece, the amount of time to complete the setup (setting up a piece of equipment), and how much tooling, if necessary, is required. A detailed estimate has the following elements:

Department	Operation Number	Set-Up Time	Production Time	Descriptions
PC	10			Issue material: $1 each
SW	20	0.5	1.0	Cut to size
BR	30	0.0	0.5	File all edges
QC	40	0.0	0.2	Inspect per Drawing #001
OP	50			Outside Processing: $0.50 each
QC	60	0.0	0 .1	Final Inspect per Drawing #001
Totals:		0.5 Hrs	1.8 Hrs	$1.50 Each (Material Cost)

In this example of a detailed estimate, the cost to make a hundred pieces has the set-up cost amortized (divided equally) over the hundred pieces. When a part requires tooling the cost is also amortized into the unit price, or listed separately as a non-recurring tooling charge (NRTC). The following calculation determines the per piece set-up cost when the fully loaded direct labor hourly rate is $10 per hour:

$10
x 0.5 = Set-Up Time
$5 ÷ 100 (pieces) = $0.05 Each

The production time total in this example is 1.8 hours for each piece. Therefore, the production time's cost is $18 (1.8 times $10 equals $18) for each piece. The following manufacturer's estimate summary is based on the detailed estimate presented above:

Material	$1.00
Outside Processing	0.50
Direct Labor	18.05
COGS	$19.55
Selling Price at 35% GP	$30.08
($19.55 ÷ 0.65 = $30.08)	

The selling price is calculated by subtracting the GP percent from 1.00 (1.00 - 0.35 = 0.65), then dividing the total cost by that result ($19.55 ÷ 0.65 equals $30.08). These are examples of a detailed estimate and summary estimate for a simple part. Many manufacturers produce parts, sub-assemblies, and assemblies that are much more complicated. Also, the complex assemblies may include purchased parts and outside processing. Therefore, the estimating process can be much more time-consuming and complicated.

Fortunately, there are many good software packages available for any size manufacturer. This was not the case when I started working and everything was done manually. However, there was one advantage to the manual method. When a mistake was made, it was usually isolated to just one part number. This is because the automatic populating (the mass adding or changing of data) of a bill of material (BOM) was not yet possible. A computer system can populate a BOM with one stroke of the enter key, one software instruction, or as a byproduct of transaction or data conversion processing.

Despite the fact that computers are extremely powerful productivity-enhancing tools, don't become seduced into believing that because it came from a computer, it's perfect. Computer programs calculate correctly, but people make mistakes. Inputting the wrong instruction into a computer system causes errors and hours of re-work. It is extremely important to compare the new software's initial outputs with the tested and proven outputs from the old software. When data is converted from one computer system to another, errors may occur. The mapping (selecting and directing) of data is a critical process in every conversion. (I know of companies whose employees spent the better part of a year—thousands of rework hours—cleaning up data conversion mapping errors!) As the man-ager, you must satisfy yourself that the new computer-generated results are correct.

Accuracy is always important. This is especially true in the area of estimating and pricing. When an error is made that creates an artificially low-cost estimate, then a low selling price is established, and some or all of your company's EBIT is lost, forever. I emphasize "forever" because new EBIT cannot replace lost EBIT. It may im-prove your company's present and future performance, but it can't do anything about the past. Furthermore, this projected loss occurred before your company even starts to make the part.

Your company may lose on the RFQ as well, because the price quoted to the customer was incorrectly high. This is why you must accurately define, calculate, and know your costs before establishing your company's selling prices.

Summary

The artistry of knowing your costs is understanding that it is the starting point for profitability. Use accurate costs in every facet of your company. Knowing costs in business is analogous to knowing costs in your personal life. For most of us, it would be unacceptable to remodel or build a home without first knowing the cost. Building your business without knowing the costs is equally unacceptable.

Costs Versus Selling Prices

The key to making money is to buy low, and sell high. If you are like me, you have probably heard people say this hundreds of times. It's an overly simplified statement about making money, but it is totally true. Sometimes as managers, we get carried away by overly complex plans and methods of implementation. We overlook the obvious message in "buy low and sell high." However, to know when you can sell high, you must know your costs.

Rarely within any company do all the items sold generate the same GP percentage. This is a byproduct of a company's dynamics, or of supply and demand. When you want to achieve an overall GP of 27 percent, but you are unable to price each item accordingly, some type of pricing system is required. Without a pricing system, you are forced to do reactive pricing rather than proactive pricing. Reactive pricing occurs after you have reviewed a report or financial statement, and observe that the pricing must be adjusted to achieve your desired results. You make price adjustments on some items, or tell your sales manager to raise prices. This is a hit-and-miss approach that can cause problems with customers, employee morale, and administration.

Pricing Systems

Several years ago I implemented a pricing system in a business group that relied on reactive pricing. There were approximately ten

101

divisions within this business group. Each division had its own reactive pricing method. The business group sold approximately twenty-five thousand different products over the course of a year. They had more than 750,000 different selling prices for those products. This condition fell within the 80/20 Pareto's Law of Distribution (80 percent of an activity, such as sales, is accounted for by 20 percent of the population, such as customers). Some products in the 80 percent activity category had over 250 unique prices.

After the pricing system was fully implemented, there were approximately a hundred thousand unique selling prices. This reduction of approximately 650,000, or 87 percent, in the number of selling prices improved the business group in several ways:

- It required much less labor to prepare an estimate for a customer, thereby improving customer service while reducing operating expenses.
- The required computer system resources were greatly reduced because of the tremendous reduction in pricing data.
- There was an improvement in GP because management had established the selling prices. Furthermore, many of the lower volume items were sold at standard pricing with no discounts!

I've found that reactive pricing is directly related to reactive selling. The salesperson asks the customer one or both of the following questions while attempting to book an order:

1. How much are you currently paying for the product?
2. What does my selling price need to be in order for me to get your business?

This is not selling; it is order taking, with the customer determining the company's GP. It also is worth noting that both of these are closed-ended questions. Therefore, reactive selling does not use the funneling selling technique I discuss in chapter twenty.

When a company has never had a pricing system before, it is a good idea to develop a simple one. The simple approach works when it's realistic for the company's industry. Making significant changes in business requires a certain amount of courage. Since changes in pricing affect customers and your sales team, it can become an emotional issue. As the manager, you must ask yourself, "Is the gain caused by the change worth the pain?" If so, then you must make the changes that will improve your company.

Customer Class Pricing

If you decide a pricing system is right for your company, explain and sell its benefits to your sales team before implementation. Selling to an internal customer—your sales team, for example—is just as important as selling to an external customer. As the manager, you are in the position of power. As tempting as it might be, don't mandate the pricing system on your sales team. This is one of those times when you should use your best selling skills to convince your salespeople that a pricing system is a good thing for everyone. By doing this you can make the conversion less painful. In one way or another, a pricing system should be implemented when you want to control your company's EBIT and GP.

When possible, keep the number of pricing classes (levels) between one and six. These classes are for your company's types of customers, products, and corresponding sales volume. For example, start by dividing your customers into three categories:

1. The A category is for customers in the top 50 percent of sales.
2. The B category is for customers in the 51 to 80 percent of sales.
3. The C category is for customers in the 81 to 100 percent of sales.

A fourth category, D is for special pricing (exceptions). The special pricing category is used when the selling price is established by the supplier, or when it requires a manager's approval. This is because the special prices are different than the supplier's or company's standard pricing. Unfortunately, "different" usually means "lower."

The following is an example of a simple pricing system I've used many times, in many companies, and in many industries. This method allows you to give each customer class a different GP percent. In this example, the management's goal is to achieve a GP of 27 percent. The projected GP percent is a result of the following calculation: Multiply the percent of total sales times the GP percent to calculate the contribution factor. The contribution factor is a customer class's contribution to the overall GP percent. Next, total the customer class' contribution factors.

Example:

Customer Class	% of Total Sales	Multiply	GP%	Contribution Factor
A	50	x	20	10.00
B	30	x	30	9.00
C	20	x	40	8.00
			Projected GP %	27.00

This model pricing system will generate a projected 27 percent GP. When the company does special pricing, what has not been taken into account is its percentage of the overall sales and its GP percentage. Once those percentages are determined, add a category to the above example for customer class D. Then recalculate the numbers for a revised projected GP percent. When the revised projected GP is not the desired 27 percent, make adjustments to the percent of total sales and GP percent categories until the desired result is achieved.

Item Class Pricing

Some of the artistry of pricing is determining where and when your company can generate an above-average GP without losing sales or market share. The easy part of developing a projected GP is doing the calculations. The difficult part is knowing what segments of your company's product offering are price sensitive. This leads to the next step in the development of a pricing system: item class pricing.

For item class pricing, use the same methodology as for the customer pricing system. Create different classes of items, and when necessary, sub-classes of items. Next, develop A, B, and C prices for every standard item sold by your company. Again, as with the customer pricing system, you may require a D category for items that have a special price. For example, a personal computer distributor would require an item class for monitors. Within the item class for monitors, they may want a sub-class for monitor suppliers and another for monitor sizes.

In many industries the original equipment manufacturers (OEM, a broad term used to describe companies that make, assemble, or add value, and brand the product with their name) publish selling price lists for end-users. When discounting is done on an item, it is accomplished by giving a discount off the list price. For example:

The IM-A-VAR Company purchases EZ2C Monitors from the WE-R-DISTI Company, a personal computer distributor. The EZ2C Monitor Company publishes a Selling Price List for the end-users. The distributor's price to the IM-A-VAR Company is 20 percent off of the EZ2C Monitor Company's selling list price. When the distributor has multiple item classes and sub-classes for different monitor categories, they are not forced to give the same discount on all monitor sales, thereby improving their gross profitability.

Fortunately, most good software packages have various methods for handling item classes, sub-item classes, and customer classes. The purpose of the pricing systems is to eliminate unnecessary discounting. In the highly competitive business world, it is a constant challenge to make a good profit. What you are attempting to avoid by using a pricing system is the loss of profits because a pricing tool is not available. There are times you may decide to take a particular piece of business below your standard requirements for profitability. Because of discounting, without having some transactions at higher than normal GP levels, it is difficult to achieve your desired overall GP results. This is especially true when the remaining transactions are selling at normal or below normal GP levels.

Pricing for OEMs and distributors are very similar. The main difference is that OEMs establish the list prices for their products. By establishing their product's list prices, they also set a benchmark, which competitors may use to determine their pricing. OEMs use several different methods for pricing their products. The decision about which pricing method the company's management selects is based in part on how it generates sales: Does it sell on a direct basis, through distribution, by using the retail channel, or can it use a combination of these options? When you manage an OEM, establish the pricing system after you have determined the best way to go to market. Don't establish your company's pricing system in a vacuum. It is important to consider your customers and competitors. This is another good example of how business involves dependent variables—not independent variables. To one degree or another, the company is dependent on the actions or reactions of the customers and competitors when it involves pricing.

Your company's selling prices and GP are directly tied to your requirement for EBIT. There is no single profitability rule for all companies. Many industrial distributors require an approximately 20 percent GP margin. This 20 percent GP covers all their operating expenses, and allows them to generate EBIT, which usually ranges between 5 and 10 percent. Large mass distributors operate on much lower margins, frequently around 10 percent GP with EBIT below 5 percent. On the opposite end of the GP and EBIT spectrum are specialty distributors. They generate a much higher GP margin, usually in excess of 50 percent, with an EBIT generally above 20 percent. The following shows why distributors and manufacturers have different financial requirements.

Example:

SUMMARY P&L

	Distributor	%	Manufacturer	%
Net Sales	$10,000,000	100.0	$10,000,000	100.0
COGS	<8,000,000>	<80.0>	<6,500,000>	<65.0>
GP	2,000,000	20.0	3,500,000	35.0
Op. Exp.	<1,000,000>	<10.0>	<1,000,000>	<10.0>
EBIT	$1,000,000	10.0	$2,500,000	25.0

SUMMARY BALANCE SHEET AND ROI CALCULATION

Inventory	$1,000.000	$1,000,000
A/R	1,500,000	1,500,000
Assets	2,000,000	8,000,000
Less; A/P	<500,000>	<500,000>
Investment	$4,000,000	$10,000,000
EBIT	$1,000,000	$2,500,000
ROI	25%	25%

As you can see in the above example, both the distributor and the manufacturer generated a 25 percent ROI. However, the manufacturer required an additional $1,500,000 of GP, because its fixed assets are $6,500,000 versus $500,000 for the distributor. These fixed assets are property, plant, and equipment, all of which are usually significantly more expensive for manufacturers than for distributors.

All actual GP levels are determined by you, your employees, your company's industry, the suppliers, and supply and demand. Whatever selling and pricing methods you select, be sure the company generates enough EBIT to meet your goals and the goals of the shareholders and employees. These goals should include your company's requirements for servicing the debt, EBT, ROE, growth in shareholders equity, research and development, and cash for future growth.

Contract Manufacturer Pricing

The pricing for contract manufacturers differs from distributors and OEMs. Since contract manufacturers are job shops, they lose, gain, or break-even on EBIT on every job they make. Contract manufacturers have an estimated GP when a customer order is booked, not a fixed percentage or dollar amount as with distributor and OEMs. Therefore, the number one rule of estimating is: Always select your most qualified employees to prepare estimates. This may sound obvious, but I've seen hundreds of contract manufacturers and the vast majority have unqualified employees doing this crucial function.

If you manage a contract manufacturer, make sure the employees doing the estimating know the capability of every piece of equipment in your plant. They also must know the capabilities of your company's employees and suppliers. Estimators must be capable of evaluating the "fit" of the parts they estimate in relation to the capabilities of your plant. This is not an easy job to fill. In many companies the estimators have more than ten years of manufacturing experience. Many managers allow the estimate to go directly to the sales manager or a less qualified employee. If you want your company to remain profitable, there are certain things you cannot delegate and establishing the selling prices is one of them. It is the best way to proactively control your company's profitability.

For managers of contract manufacturers, it is essential to know what is the "perfect part" for your company. Perfect part means it is most profitable for your company to manufacture. Some qualifications to consider are the part's complexity, customer, delivery schedule, material, quantity, size, and tolerances. Obviously, all the parts a company estimates, quotes, and manufactures are not going to match the perfect part profile 100 percent. However, when approximately 80 percent of a company's sales are generated by making perfect parts, with accurate estimates and selling prices, then the desired EBIT is achieved. When the perfect parts represent only 20 percent of a company's sales, the manager has a major problem. Either the sales force is focused on the wrong customers, or they are calling on the right customers but getting RFQs for the wrong parts. (In chapter seventeen I discuss the "perfect customer," which is directly related to the perfect part.)

If a manufacturer is in a downward business cycle, one possible reason may be that the company is partially or completely obsolete.

When this is the case, one must ask how it happened. Often, I've seen this problem caused by the mistaken decision to manufacture everything in-house. Acquiring equipment usually limits a company. Some managers and employees with strong manufacturing backgrounds believe they must make everything in-house. In most cases, the life of a piece of equipment is between three to ten years. Therefore, the company is restricted to that capability for some period of time. When technology changes, the company may own a piece of equipment that is obsolete. Because of this business dynamic, I have found it is better to do in-house only what is absolutely essential for the ongoing success of the company and out-source everything else. This will increase the odds of the company remaining profitable, surviving, and becoming more flexible in the process.

Contract manufacturers require a higher GP and EBIT percentage than the average distributor. This is partially because their downside risks are greater. For managers of contract manufacturers, I suggest targeting for a minimum GP of 35 percent and a minimum EBIT target of 20 percent. There are two exceptions to these general guidelines:

1. When the company is a high-volume, long-run contract manufacturer, I've used a target GP as low as 25 percent and an EBIT target of 15 percent.

2. When the company is a low-volume, short-run contract manufacturer, I've used minimum targets of 50 percent for GP and 25 percent for EBIT. This is because the learning curve on short-run parts must be equally short, as the company may never get another order to make that part.

These ranges of GP and EBIT are another dynamic of the contract manufacturer, because:

1. High-volume, long-run contract manufacturers generally have very expensive equipment and tooling, and less expensive direct labor employees.

2. Low-volume, short-run contract manufacturers usually have less expensive equipment and tooling, and more expensive direct labor forces.

Every contract manufacturing company is different. You must establish targets for your company based on your company's cost structure. However, whatever GP and EBIT targets you establish must meet or exceed your target for ROI!

Summary

The artistry of pricing for distributors and manufacturers involves knowing your costs, preparing accurate estimates, and establishing fair and profitable selling prices for your company's products and services. No matter what type of business you're in, mastering the artistry of pricing is one of the cornerstones to achieving controlled profitable growth. The artistry of pricing for contract manufacturers lies in establishing selling prices from accurate estimates, so a high percentage of the customer's orders meet or exceed your GP and EBIT goals. A percentage of parts contract manufacturers make become "losers"—parts the company loses money on during the manufacturing process. Since contract manufacturers make parts for other companies, they can't control the part's life cycle. They never know if, or when, they will receive a repeat order for any part. Therefore, it is very important to make the most money on these parts as possible, the first time they manufacture it. This is accomplished by having most of the company's sales generated from manufacturing perfect parts.

Return on Investment: Inventory, Accounts Receivable, Accounts Payable, and Fixed Assets

One of the most common measurements of a company's performance is return on investment (ROI), or return on equity (ROE). This measurement shows a company's return in relation to its investment. Usually, ROI is used in relation to EBIT and EBT. ROE is generally used to describe the return generated by a company on a net income (after tax) basis.

The ROI generated by a company is in part related to the EBIT. The EBIT results allow you to know how your company is doing in relation to net sales. On financial statements, net sales are always presented as 100 percent. Every other category on the financial statement is expressed in relation to net sales.

Example:

Gross Sales	$102.00	102%
Less Discounts and Allowances	<2.00>	<2%>
Net Sales	$100.00	100%
Cost of Goods Sold	<65.00>	<65%>
GP	$35.00	35%
Less Operating Expenses	<15.00>	<15%>
EBIT	$20.00	20%

111

To analyze a company's financial performance, you must know how much is invested in the company. When a company earns $1 million of EBIT and has an average annual investment of $2 million, it's generating a 50 percent ROI. However, when a company makes the same $1 million of EBIT, but the average annual investment is $10 million, it's only generating a 10 percent ROI. As a manager or investor, you are always trying to generate the maximum ROI. Therefore, your goal is to earn the highest rate of return from the investment in your company. But this return should always be in relation to the amount of risk you and your shareholders can tolerate.

Generating a company's ROI is the responsibility of the manager. Since 1975, I set an hourly rate on what my time had to generate in terms of EBIT. Recently, I had responsibility for generating $25 million of annual EBIT. This equals $2,083,333 per month, $480,769 per week, $96,154 per work day, and $12,019 per hour. As an ROI test, I asked myself the following question several times during the course of most work days: Will what I'm doing right now generate $12,000 of EBIT per hour for the company over the course of the next three years? When my answer was yes, I would continue to be involved in that situation. But when my answer was no, I would do something else that was a more profitable use of my time.

Obviously, there are certain mandatory job functions that you can't generate this type of return or any return at all. However, when the majority of your time is not involved in generating EBIT and improving the ROI for your company, you should evaluate how you spend your time. When you don't set the proper management example of using your time productively, you will inadvertently send the wrong message to your employees. In business, time is money. To waste it is the same as throwing away your company's hard-earned profits.

Inventory

Before starting this discussion on inventory management, I'll tell you about my first experience managing inventory. At the age of twenty, I managed the clothing department for a now-defunct California-based department store named The Akron. At the time, it was a successful business and had been for many years. They ran very artistic newspaper ads twice a week advertising low-priced, well-designed imported merchandise. In fact, their home furnishings were so popular they were referred to as "early Akron" when describing their appearance from a decorating perspective.

Everyone who worked for The Akron started in the warehouse. One of the reasons for their success was the use of some just-in-time (JIT) practices. This was done long before JIT was being used by many U.S. companies. Every day large trucks would arrive at the warehouse docks. It was the warehouse employee's job to unload the trucks and move the merchandise to the selling floor as fast as possible. Typically, it took one hour to unload a truck and two hours to stock the merchandise. The Akron operated like a grocery store. This experience taught me some of the JIT principals, literally from the warehouse floor, up.

The clothing department at The Akron did not work on a JIT basis. It worked on an MIIB (more inventory is better) basis. Historically, the clothing department had two inventories. One inventory was "floor" inventory, meaning it was available for sale. The other inventory was "store" inventory, meaning it was in the warehouse as backup inventory for the floor inventory. The store inventory made perfect sense to me, for it was the fast-moving items that could not be replenished between standard deliveries. Standard deliveries were on a weekly basis. But having store inventory for the slow-moving items with standard deliveries made no sense to me at all.

During my first month as manager of the clothing department, I started reducing the store inventory on slow-moving items. That same month, the clothing manager for all of The Akron stores paid me a visit. I explained what I was doing to him and why I was doing it. He didn't get it. This was mainly because when he managed an Akron store's clothing department, he didn't do it that way. Within three months I reduced the store inventory products by approximately 80 percent. Every month the clothing manager visited me, and we would have this same discussion. I told him how much the inventory was reduced, how much faster I had done my purchasing, and taking the physical (counting) inventory. He still didn't understand. He actually thought I was a little lazy because I completed my work in less time. Out of pure frustration and my need to get another opinion, I explained what I was doing to the store's general manager. He didn't get it either. I believed what I was doing was right, even though I had no formal education or experience in inventory management at that time. I could not waste the company's money on excess inventory and labor. But the managers I worked for didn't seem to care about or understand ROI and proper inventory management.

I have looked back at this situation many times and consider it one of my most valuable learning experiences. I had to satisfy myself that what I was doing was right, or if it was wrong, then I needed to find out why. The Akron managers couldn't explain why their method was superior; they simply insisted it be done their way. I generated greatly improved results for the company. But the company's management wanted their method used, more than they wanted improved results—style over substance was their preference. I knew it was time for me to move on, and I resigned as a direct result of my conflict with management over this issue.

Since inventory is one of a company's major investments, you should know how much return on inventory investment (ROII) is required to cover the operating expenses and to break-even. The "return" in ROII is the GP dollars generated. When a company has an average inventory investment of $1 million, and generates $500,000 annually in GP dollars, the ROII is 50 percent ($500,000 ÷ $1,000,000 = 50 %). The larger the company's investment in inventory, the more GP dollars are required to yield the desired return. Therefore, the higher the ROII the better, as long as the service level is being met or exceeded.

When a company's annual operating expenses are $1,200,000, and the average inventory investment is $1 million, the company requires a 120 percent ROII, or $1,200,000, in GP to break-even.

Example:

Annualized Operating Expenses	$1,200,000	
Average Inventory Investment	$1,000,000	= 120 Percent Break-Even ROII

Remember, the above example shows what is required to break-even, not what is required to generate a positive ROI or ROII. When a company has an ROI goal of 25 percent and a total investment of $3 million, it must earn $750,000 of EBIT ($3,000,000 times 25 percent equals $750,000). The greater the total investment and inventory investment, the higher the ROII target must be to generate the required ROI. The following shows two companies with the same operating expenses but different average inventory investments.

Example:

	Company A	Company B
Average Non-inventory Investment	$2,000,000	$2,000,000
Average Inventory Investment	$1,000,000	$2,000,000
Total Investment	$3,000,000	$4,000,000
GP required for a 25% ROI	$ 750,000	$1,000,000
Annualized Operating Expenses	$1,200,000	$1,200,000
ROII $ Required for a 25% ROI	$1,950,000	$2,200,000
ROII % Achieved with a 25% ROI	195%	110%

As you can see, Company A is generating a better ROII than Company B. Be sure the employees who manage your company's inventory understand this calculation and that it's their responsibility to generate the required ROII. Also, have the computerized measurement programs, screens, and reports in place so the results are reported on an ad hoc, monthly, prior-ninety-day, quarterly, year-to-date, and annual basis. When the required ROII is not generated, the employees responsible for managing the inventory must find out what is causing the problem and fix it.

Some managers make a common mistake when trying to correct excess inventory problems in their companies. The first thing they do is limit the amount of inventory their buyers can purchase. Since, by definition, the top-moving items represent a high percentage of sales, they also represent a high percentage of purchases. Therefore, this approach only further compounds the excess inventory problem because the company's buyers are not properly replenishing the inventory that sells the most. This may seem basic, but some managers are looking for quick-fix solutions to problems. For them, it is much easier to mandate reducing monthly purchases by a certain percentage or dollar amount, than taking the necessary time to properly resolve the problem. If your company has an excess inventory problem, do a Gap Analysis (see pages 63 and 184) and corresponding Action Item List (see pages 150 and 179). Remember: Customer Service begins by having the right inventory, in the right quantities, in available-for-sale condition. The first rule of fixing an excess inventory problem is: Don't stop purchasing the good-moving inventory!

I learned this first rule of fixing inventory problems in 1968 from Manny Krupin, General Manager of a distribution company. I was a part-time truck driver. Every so often, I delivered boxes of financial paperwork from the division where I worked to Manny's division. During one of my deliveries, Manny said: "Young man, please come over here. I want to have a talk with you."

My first thought was I had put the boxes in the wrong place or Manny had seen me driving away in the truck too fast. Instead, he asked me into his office and told me to sit down. Then he proceeded to tell me the following: "You appear to be a bright, very hard-working young man. So every time you come to my division, I want to give you some golden rules of business. Now, the first rule of fixing an inventory problem is...." Instantly Manny became one of my mentors, especially during my truck driver days when he shared his knowledge with me.

A company's software package should measure and report the ROII results by buyer, supplier, item class, sub-item class, product, company location, total company, and customer. By having the ROII results reported this way, it is easy to see who and what are performing better, and who and what are causing the problems. When the excess inventory problem is recurring—or worse, perpetual—review the software's material management module. Perhaps the purchasing formula is incorrectly set. The more sophisticated software packages have a standard feature that compares a company's actual inventory results to projected inventory results, if other purchasing formulas had been used. These systems will automatically recommend one or more purchasing formulas that will generate improved ROII results.

Sometimes it's impossible to achieve the desired ROII on a particular supplier's product, item class, or sub-class of products. When this occurs, share the information with the supplier to determine if there is another way to improve the ROII. Perhaps there is more GP available, or your company may be able to support the product line with less inventory. When a product line consistently generates a lower than required ROII, you may be forced to switch to a competing supplier's products. However, this should be done as a last resort and only after every way of improving the ROII has been thoroughly investigated. Long-term relationships with suppliers are just as important as any other significant business relationship.

Accounts Receivable

Another important factor in determining a company's ROI is the management of A/R, the customer's unpaid invoices for the selling company's products and services. The company's payment terms are printed on their invoices. The invoice payment terms, such as "2 percent 10 days, net 30 days," are to a large extent determined by the payment terms your company's industry offers its customers.

When your company can vary from the industry's standard invoice terms or from what the larger customers dictate, it is easier to establish your own invoice terms. Generally, to collect the A/R faster, offer a significant discount. By significant, I mean to say that when customers calculate your company's invoice discount terms, they determine that they make more money paying your invoice, than their cost of money or target for ROI.

What is the actual cost to a company when it offers a 1, 2, or 3 percent discount for payment within ten days? When customers pay a company's invoices within ten days and the invoice terms are "1 percent 10 days, net 30 days," the discount taken costs the selling company approximately 18 percent per year. This is because there are approximately eighteen twenty-day periods in a 365-day year (18 x 1 % = 18 %), and the invoice is being paid 20 days sooner. As the seller, you must determine what invoice terms make economic sense for your company. The discounts taken by customers directly reduce the company's EBIT. Most customers have their own methods for determining when it makes financial sense to take an invoice's discount. From the seller's perspective, periodically survey your customers to determine what discount terms are being taken. Then make any necessary adjustments to your company's invoice terms.

The management of a company's A/R is the direct responsibility of the credit manager. The time to collect and the percentage of A/R collected are reliant on having the right credit manager, employees, software, and industry. Time in A/R is measured by the number of average day's sales outstanding (DSO). Percentage in A/R is expressed as the percent of the A/R total that is collected, or the percent of the A/R total that is written off (not collected).

Credit Managers

This position requires diverse skills. It is part accountant, asset manager, enforcer, risk analyst, and salesperson. Unfortunately, often credit managers and their employees are viewed as being in conflict with the sales force. Nothing should be further from the truth. The credit department's employees should work with the salespeople and with customers to ensure the company's A/Rs are collected per the invoice terms. The results achieved in managing a company's A/R are enhanced when employees from the credit and sales departments work together. This is why it is so important to have the right person as your credit manager.

Every company, no matter how large they are, has finite resources. It is imperative that these resources are utilized to the fullest extent. In the final analysis, most companies are ultimately selling their time. A company's time is charged in various methods. It may be on an hourly basis for services rendered or as part of a product's selling price. The main function of the credit department's employees is to use their finite time collecting the company's finite money. Their goal should be to spend their time with customers who are creditworthy and pay according to the company's invoice terms.

Some good customers take the discount and pay within ten days. Other good customers take the discount and pay after ten days. Some other good customers, who don't take the discount, will take more than the maximum allowable number of days to pay an invoice. This is where the judgment of the credit manager comes into play. He or she must know the difference between slow-paying creditworthy customers and slow-paying non-creditworthy customers. Remember from chapter nine that the business cycle ends when the customer's payment clears the seller's bank. To expedite the process of receiving cash, you can use electronic funds transfers from your customer's banks to your company's bank.

When you're constantly involved with credit decisions, you either have the wrong credit manager or you have usurped their authority. The credit manager, directly or indirectly, interfaces with every department, customer, and supplier of a company. Unless your company is in a financially strong industry, it's going to incur some bad debt write-offs. When a company that generates a 10 percent EBIT writes off a $10,000 bad debt, it requires an additional $100,000 in sales to get back to zero. Excess bad debt write-offs, just like excess expenses or investments, can slow or eliminate a company's ability to grow. Therefore, the credit manager must be someone who is also pro-growth and makes sure the growth is with creditworthy customers. The goal of the credit manager is to maximize the reward while minimizing the risk of the company's investment in A/R.

Accounts Payable

The corresponding transaction to one company's A/R, is another company's A/P. A technique I used many times to improve the ROI was to contact the suppliers who offered invoice discount percents for prompt payment below what one of my divisions or business groups were taking. When we were taking all discounts greater than "2 percent 10 days, net 30 days," I would have the controller contact every supplier who was offering lower discount terms. The controller would tell the suppliers that if they offered our company a 2 percent discount for payments made within ten days, we would pay within ten days. The first time I tried this, I was amazed when most of the suppliers took us up on our offer. What amazed me even more was when some suppliers said if we paid them on a cash on delivery (COD) basis, they would give the company a 5 percent discount! The difference between these discounts and the company's cost of money goes straight to the bottom line. Obviously, a company must be in a strong cash position to create opportunities such as these.

Fixed Assets

If contemplating a capital expenditure (Cap-X), an estimated ROI statement must be prepared. For example, your company requires a new piece of equipment that costs $500,000. Your company's minimum ROI criteria is 25 percent. The first step in preparing the estimate is determining how much additional EBIT should be generated by this investment. Also determine how much the labor, material, outside processing, and operating expenses will be reduced by this new piece of equipment. In order to financially justify this Cap-X, your company must generate an additional $125,000 per year of EBIT ($500,000 x 25 % = $125,000). This financial analysis should be done for every potential fixed asset investment that is depreciable (written-off over time) based on the Internal Revenue Service's guidelines.

Once the new fixed asset is received and posted in your company's fixed assets ledger, begin measuring the results. Measure the actual results versus estimated results on every fixed asset investment. When this isn't done, it's impossible to know which of your investment decisions are generating the expected ROIs. After the learning curve on a new piece of equipment is completed, the results should meet or exceed the estimated ROI. When the results are below the projected ROI, it's time for another Gap Analysis.

Unfortunately, some managers fall into a trap by believing it's too time-consuming to measure every fixed asset investment. Fortunately, this doesn't have to be the case. Companies with software of average sophistication can easily calculate the ROI for any investment. For that matter, this calculation can be done with a basic manual cost accounting system. The important objective is to isolate the expenses, GP, investment, and sales from the other equipment in the company.

Improving the ROI

The three primary ways to improve a company's ROI are:

1. Reduce the investment.
2. Improve the EBIT.
3. A combination of both. The following illustrates this.

Example:

	Base Case	Investment	EBIT	Both
Net Sales	$10,000,000	$10,000,000	$10,000,000	$10,000,000
Inventory	1,000,000	250,000	1,000,000	250,000
A/R	1,000,000	250,000	1,000,000	250,000
Fixed Assets	$1,000,000	$1,000,000	$1,000,000	$1,000,000
Average Investment	$3,000,000	$1,500,000	$3,000,000	$1,500,000
EBIT $	1,000,000	1,000,000	2,000,000	2,000,000
EBIT %	10%	10%	20%	20%
ROI %	33%	67%	67%	133%

In this example, a decrease in the average investment of $1,500,000 is required to achieve a 67 percent ROI. The same 67 percent ROI can also be achieved by increasing the EBIT by $1 million. Therefore, the best way to improve a company's ROI is to improve EBIT and simultaneously reduce the average investment. In this example, the combined improvement would generate a 133 percent ROI ($2,000,000 ÷ $1,500,000 = 133 %).

Now, if you manage a manufacturing company that has long-run jobs (typically the term used when referring to jobs that run for months or years, versus days or weeks), you can really maximize your company's ROI by using a full-blown JIT system. In a JIT environment, the company buys from certified suppliers (see page 129), and can have their material delivered to the point-of-use (POU). POU means the material goes directly from the receiving dock to where it is used in the manufacturing or assembly process. There is no receiving inspection and no store inventory. Literally, a company can turn its inventory more than 365 times per year. Because, depending on the production volume, material can be delivered one or more times during the day. Using the above example of a $10 million company, where the company has a COGS of 70 percent, a one-day supply of inventory is $19,178. The company's ROI would be 158 percent ($10,000,000 ÷ 365 = $27,397. $27,397 x 70 % COGS = $19,178 Average Days Sales at Cost. $2,000,000 EBIT ÷ $1,269,178 =158 % ROI) when it can operate with a one-day supply of material.

Summary

The artistry of managing accounts receivable, fixed assets, and inventory is in achieving an above-average EBIT, ROE, ROI and ROII over a long period of time. As stated in chapters eleven and twelve, you must know your costs and establish proper selling prices to properly manage your company's EBIT, ROE, ROI, and ROII. Whenever you are considering a significant investment, prepare an estimated ROI statement. If the investment is made, measure the actual versus the estimated results. When the results are below the projected ROI, do a Gap Analysis.

Reducing
Transaction Labor and
Continuous Improvement

CHAPTER FOURTEEN

There are many ways to make money in business. Three ways are:

1. Increasing sales
2. Increasing the GP
3. Decreasing operating expenses

When a company's sales are $10 million at 25 percent GP with a 10 percent EBIT and the operating expenses are reduced from 15 percent to 14 percent, the EBIT increases to 11 percent. This is equal to a 10 percent improvement in EBIT (1.0 ÷ 10.0 = 10 percent), or $100,000. To achieve the same $100,000 improvement in EBIT by increasing sales with an EBIT of 10 percent, the company's sales would have to increase by $1 million ($100,000 ÷ 10 % = $1,000,000).

Increasing sales, increasing the GP, and reducing the operating expenses are all good and necessary ways to improve the EBIT. Which is best? Well, there's more than one answer. An increase in sales requires additional investments in A/R, employees, inventory, and perhaps fixed assets. I've found that it's better to reduce operating expenses and increase the GP. But the best way is to do all three!

In today's highly competitive business environment, managers must continuously examine and improve all processes. Improving

123

means reducing the company's costs of labor, investments, materials, and outside processing, while improving the company's products, services, sales, and market share. One of the tenets of TQM is continuous improvement. Therefore, TQM should be a part of every company's culture.

Whatever you and your employees do today will not be good enough for tomorrow. The better you and your employees have designed and implemented the company's processes, the less redesigning will be required. But no matter how good the design was at a given point in time, improvements in technology and competition necessitate change. Change is a constant we must all accept.

In a seller's market, when demand is outpacing supply, customers may unknowingly pay for a supplier's inefficiencies. They may require the products or services so badly, the selling prices become of secondary importance. But in a buyer's market, when supply is more abundant than demand, most customers won't pay for a supplier's inefficiencies. And why should they? Today there are so many good suppliers and so many easy ways to purchase from them, it is truly a buyer's market.

A prime example of why continuous improvement is so important is the Volkswagen Beetle. In the 1960s, it caught the world by storm because of its initial and ongoing low cost of driving and maintenance. With some modifications, the car basically remained the same for the next two decades. Production was eventually stopped because of decreasing sales and increased competition.

Flash forward: On the cover of *Motor Trend* magazine for February 1999 is the announcement that Volkswagen's New Beetle is their Import Car of the Year for 1999. Quite a turnaround for a car that was basically dead. The message in this example is that continuous improvements may have allowed the VW Bug continuing success, rather than forcing a complete redesign.

There are several analysis techniques and subsequent actions required to reduce the labor content in a company's processes.

1. Do a process flow analysis of your company's entire order fulfillment cycle. A process flow analysis is the charting or mapping of an operation, process or transaction. This analysis identifies the existing sequence of operations required to do a function— order entry, for example. Evaluate the results to determine if there are redundant operations. If so, eliminate them.

2. Often the redundancies are easier to see when you are an out-sider. Several years ago, when one of my responsibilities was the IT department, two of my best employees and I visited the company's largest distributor division to do an operational analysis. The IT department's installation team had recently completed a software conversion at this division with the company's proprietary distribution package. The normal software conversion learning curve was completed, and it was time to see how much the new software would allow the employees to improve the division's performance. We spent one week at the division, interviewing most of the employees to learn how they did their work and why. At the end of each day, the three of us met to compare notes and discuss what we had learned. During one of these meetings we learned that the division had two departments, with approximately ten employees each, doing exactly the same function. Again, because the division was the company's largest, and had grown very rapidly without having the proper software package, they were unable to control their growth. The bottom line to this story is the division was able to do the same amount of work with 50 fewer employees. They went from 185 employees to 135 employees—a 27 percent reduction. I don't like to see good employees terminated, but this excess payroll had to be dealt with immediately. The changes we implemented at the company's largest distributor division made it the largest generator of EBIT as well.

3. List the transactions and operations performed by your employees in ranked order, with the largest users of labor hours first. Then analyze what is required to reduce the labor content in each operation, starting with the largest users of labor hours. This analysis can be accomplished in several ways. I've found better results occur when employees who work together do the analysis and develop their own action item plans. This is because they have a vested interest in the results. They know they will reap the rewards of their efforts on a daily basis, since the changes they make improve their jobs. Also, they are probably the most knowledgeable employees about the real requirements of the operations, processes, and transactions being analyzed. This analysis method may be necessary when your company has new software. This is because sometimes when companies install new software, the employees continue to do

their work the same old way. They have not reengineered their jobs to take advantage of the labor savings the new software made possible. When the ROI estimate was prepared to justify the Cap-X for the new software, more than likely the majority of the return came from estimated labor savings. When your employees don't have the necessary reengineering skills, a consultant should be retained to help with this process. I believe you will find this is money well spent. The consultant should thoroughly understand the software and be familiar with your company's type of business. Many software companies pride themselves on the belief that their product provides "best practices" methods. Best practices methods means the operation, process, or transaction is done in the very best way possible (the lowest cost and the highest quality). Therefore, when you investigate potential software providers, include the best practices service as part of your RFQ. When your company has had the software for a number of years, ask the provider for a post-installation best practices evaluation. In either case, request a fixed-fee or not-to-exceed proposal.

4. Use the backlog of customer orders to determine future labor requirements. When your company has a backlog of orders, determine what the relation is between your backlog and your labor requirements. The following examples explain how to calculate this for distributors and manufacturers:

Calculation for Distributors

For distributors who receive scheduled customer orders, calculate the GP dollar value of the backlog. Usually, calculating one quarter's backlog in thirty-day, sixty-day, and ninety-day categories is sufficient. Next determine how much book-ship or turns (non-backordered customer's orders that ship from the distributor's available-for-sale inventory) business your company averages per month. Then review the previous three years of your company's sales and backlog to determine the historical book-ship relation. This review shows any trends or special occurrences that have impacted your company's book-ship relation. The following example explains how to determine the labor content of your company's backlog:

	GP $
90 Days of Customer's Backlog Orders	$100,000
90 Days of Historical Book-Ship Sales	$ 20,000
Total	$120,000

In this example, the next ninety-day period is projected to generate $120,000 of GP. I've found that it's more useful to establish a payroll target as a percentage of GP, rather than as a percentage of net sales. This is because there is a more important relation between the EBIT and GP than there is between the EBIT and net sales. In this example, your company's payroll expense target is 30 percent of the GP. Therefore, the budget for the next ninety days is $36,000, or $12,000 per month ($120,000 x 30 % = $36,000. $36,000 ÷ 3 = $12,000). When your current monthly payroll is $18,000, there is an excess payroll problem of $6,000 per month. There may be justifiable reasons to spend 50 percent of your company's GP for payroll. But when this is not the case, it is better to proactively deal with the projected excess payroll problem by restructuring your company to match reality.

Calculation for Manufacturers

The calculation for determining the relation between labor requirements, backlog, and GP is very similar for manufacturers. The main difference lies in measuring the backlog in terms of direct labor hours. To accomplish this, subtract the raw material, outside processing, and manufacturing burden expenses from your company's backlog of GP dollars. The result from this calculation is the GP dollars available for the direct labor portion of your company's backlog. The remainder of the calculation is the same as for distributors. One very important thing to remember when you review the results from this calculation: The result is your company's future direct labor requirement only, not your total payroll requirement. For manufacturers, there is a relation between direct labor and indirect labor. The manufacturing burden includes the indirect labor engineers, production controllers, operations managers, and plant managers. Every manufacturer has its own ratio for direct labor to indirect labor, as there is no standard ratio. When you make adjustments to the direct labor portion of the payroll, be sure to evaluate the indirect labor payroll as well. When the ratio between direct and indirect labor changes dramatically in a negative way, it will impact the GP and EBIT. By "negative way," this means that when the direct to indirect labor payroll ratio was 2.0 to 1.0, and because of direct labor changes it becomes 1.0 to 1.0. When this occurs, the manufacturing burden percent increases, since it is measured in relation to direct labor. Therefore, this condition causes your company's current selling hourly rate to increase. Also, because a lower selling hourly rate was used during estimating, the parts currently being made have less GP. Again, be proactive and structure to match reality.

Example:

DIRECT LABOR TO MANUFACTURING BURDEN RATIO

	2.0 to 1.0	1.0 to 1.0
Manufacturing Burden	$100,000	$100,000
Direct Labor	$200,000	$100,000
Manufacturing Burden Rate	50 %	100 %
Selling Hourly Rate When		
Direct Labor $10 per Hour	$15	$20

It is important to note that a negative change in the direct to indirect payroll ratio and corresponding manufacturing burden rate may not cause a reduction in GP. For example, your company has a monthly direct labor expense and manufacturing burden expense of $200,000 and $100,000, respectively. Therefore, the direct labor expense and the manufacturing burden ratio is 2.0 to 1.0, with a manufacturing burden rate of 50.0 percent. Your company acquires a new piece of equipment that allow it to manufacture the same amount of product with $100,000 less direct labor payroll per month. This change causes the direct labor expense to manufacturing burden expense ratio to change to 1.0 to 1.0. and the manufacturing burden rate to become 100 percent. The ratio has changed in a negative way, but the GP has changed in a positive way by $100,000. As we know, the GP is more important than a ratio and in this example made your company more EBIT.

This analysis method is especially helpful for managers who have only been in growth modes. Because of this positive condition, chances are they never had to deal with excess payroll problems. Unfortunately, I've dealt with this problem many times. What I learned from these experiences is to have fewer employees working more hours. For example, whenever possible I had the hourly employees work fifty hours per week. By using this approach, I could reduce the payroll expense by simply reducing the number of hours the employees worked per week. Therefore, I was able to accomplish a payroll reduction without having to terminate valuable employees. I viewed the cost for this flexibility as minimal, in relation to the benefits to the company, employees, management, and shareholders. There's only a 10 percent premium for this approach (40 hours x $10 per hour = $400. Ten hours of overtime is 10 x $10 = $100 x 1.5 overtime premium equals $150. $400 + $150 = $550 ÷ 50 hours = $11 per hour. $11 - $10 = $1. $1 ÷ $10 equals 10%, or a 10% premium). Also, by having a standard work week of fifty hours, I could balance the supply (labor) and demand (backlog of customer orders) more effectively for the company.

5. Outsource your company's work. In manufacturing terms, this is a make or buy decision. When it is less expensive to have certain work done by another company, and it won't negatively impact customer service or quality, outsource it. Companies should only do work in-house that is cost-effective and absolutely essential. If you decide to outsource some of your company's work, you will need a supplier quality assurance program. This program is essential to ensure your company's supplier's products and services meet or exceed your customer's requirements. Your company's quality assurance manager certifies those suppliers whose products and service are used without source (at the supplier's location) or receiving inspection.

Continuous Improvement should be a part of every company's culture. Whenever I look at my characteristics as a manager, I believe I was blessed and cursed with the same trait. No matter how well the company was running, I always wanted it to run better. I relentlessly pursued perfection because I focused on what was possible rather than what was impossible. I didn't see barriers. Instead, I saw opportunities. I always viewed continuous improvement as a natural part of all features of life. Charles Darwin named this process "natural selection," which is more commonly referred to as "survival of the fittest."

One of the most powerful examples of this evolutionary process is in the semiconductor industry. There is a term called Moore's Law. Moore's Law states that every eighteen months the computing power of a semiconductor doubles, with no increase in cost. We have all benefitted from this dynamic, as many of the non-perishable items we purchase use some type of semiconductor device. This is especially true with PCs, where the constantly improving "bang for the buck" relation is so apparent. Recently, I heard the next generation of semiconductors will be a hundred times more powerful than today's devices. Will this make Moore's Law obsolete? Perhaps. Again, the important point is that being a best-in-class company requires being better in the future than you are today.

Earlier, I quoted an article from an unknown source. The following is another such article. This article clearly explains the process of becoming the best. Here are the unknown author's "Seven Steps to Being the Best":

1. Determine the world standard. Odds are you're already benchmarking (Note: Benchmarking is an improvement process in which a company measures its performance against that of best-in-class companies, determines how those companies achieved their performance levels, and uses the information to improve its own performance.). If not, get cracking. Do not limit your surveys to your industry. Find the world champion in every process you measure, from inventory turns to customer service.

2. Use process mapping. Break down your organization's activities into component parts. Identify the inefficiencies, then redesign each process as if from scratch. For each step, ask whether customers would pay for it if they knew about it.

3. Communicate with your employees as if your life depended on it. Get your people focused on external customers and competitors. Define a clear vision that creates a sense of urgency. Help them understand the impact of their own behavior.

4. Distinguish what needs to be done from how hard the doing of it might be. Do not let difficulty daunt you. If something really needs to be done, the difficulty of doing it is irrelevant.

5 Set stretch targets. There is nothing wrong with asking your people to perform as well as the best in the world. Do not tell them how to do it, though; their ideas will be better than yours. Do not punish people for failing to reach stretch targets.

6. Never stop. When you get ahead of the pack, you will want to relax. That's just when they are becoming energized by benchmarking against you.

7. Pay attention to you inner self. You cannot win if you are dead of a heart attack or maddened by stress. So exercise. Meditate. Make love. Build a tree house. Do something selfless. Global competition demands the best of you. Becoming centered has never been more important.

One way I found to keep focused on continuously reducing transaction labor is to think of it as complementing, and not cloning, work. This may be the work of customers, employees, or suppliers. When functions are done redundantly, they add costs without adding value. This concept was discussed in detail in the preceding chapter.

Summary

The artistry of reducing the labor in every transaction and continuous improvement is the relentless pursuit of perfection by you and your employees. This is accomplished by using the tools of Total Quality Management every day, forever. Being the best at anything is never easy, but it is achievable with desire, knowledge, and working intelligently. Having good luck and good timing also helps!

Complement, Don't Clone

Have you ever watched a baseball game in which two players trying to catch a fly ball smash into one another, miss the ball, fall to the ground, and semi-consciously watch the opposing team's base runner slides easily into home plate as the umpire yells "Safe"? Well, if you've seen such a sight, then you've seen an example of cloning, not complementing activities.

Complement, don't clone, is a phrase I use to describe a principle that applies to every feature of business. All employees must contribute value to their company's products and services, not add unnecessary costs. In manufacturing there is an old saying: "Two people, one machine, doesn't make money." Obviously, there are exceptions to this statement. But the point of the saying is to emphasize the benefit of having the fewest number of employees doing the most amount of work. One way to achieve this is by complementing and not cloning your customers, employees, and suppliers.

An approach I've used since my college days as an art student has been to design something with a single element, and then challenge myself to avoid adding a second element, unless it was absolutely necessary. I use this for new ventures and for evaluating existing employees, departments, and companies. By using this approach you can maintain or return your company to a mean-and-lean condition.

When distributors and the suppliers they represent offer the same services to the same customers, they are cloning and not comple-

133

menting one another. For example, when a supplier that sells through distribution has a local demo center that is not utilized 100 percent, is it necessary for their distributors to have demo centers in the same marketplace? No. The supplier and their distributors should use one demo center. Should suppliers and their distributors provide technical support to the same customers? No. The main purpose of distribution is to sell and service the customers who are too small for the suppliers to sell and service directly.

In business news, one company is generating a lot of coverage because of its results and business model: Dell Computer Corporation. Dell sells everything on a direct basis. Therefore, they don't clone functions with distributors or value-added resellers (VARs). They are one of the fastest growing and most profitable companies in business today. Recently, several of their competitors announced plans to partially or completely follow the Dell business model. Having 100 percent of a company's sales done on a direct basis isn't new. What is new is that Dell is using best practices methods for getting its products and services to customers. Sales are generated by toll-free telephone numbers, e-commerce, and a direct sales force.

As a manager, when I saw more than one employee doing one task, I would ask why. I often found that the task was poorly designed and planned. Therefore, it required excess labor to make. I examine my participation in business meetings the same way. Anytime I participate in a meeting, I look around the room to determine if my attendance is required. When I believe I can't add enough value to the meeting, I leave and go do something more productive. My departure sets the proper productivity example, because when a company is properly structured, the employees always have plenty of work to do. If they're not required at a meeting, then they too will take the opportunity to leave. Another benefit from this approach is that the company's meetings become much more productive. They have more appropriate attendance, frequency, and purpose.

Meetings with a room full of employees are expensive. To put this cost in financial perspective, consider the following: Ten employees attend a four-hour meeting. The employees average compensation is $100,000 per year. Therefore, the hourly expense to the company is approximately $50 per hour per employee, or $2,000 for the four-hour meeting. If the company's payroll target is 25 percent of the GP, the four-hour meeting should produce $8,000 of additional GP from $32,000 in new sales. I think you get the picture. (However, don't so get carried away with this approach to the point that you start bringing a calculator to every meeting.)

In chapter thirteen I briefly addressed the importance of establishing an hourly rate for your time. When you establish an hourly rate for your time and for the time of your employees, you can quickly determine if an endeavor is economically worthwhile. There are going to be certain times when this concept won't apply at all. That's okay, because this is a general guideline about the employee's productivity. Like any general rule, be sure you temper it with a healthy dose of common sense. Remember, general rules are generally accurate and may be specifically inaccurate.

Two of a company's most important complementary relationships exist with its "perfect customer" and "perfect supplier" (see chapters seventeen and eighteen). These successful companies may not refer to their customers as "perfect," but they are their most valued customers and as such, are essential to the company's growth and survival. But you must first determine if your company is the right size for its market and industry, which I discuss in the next chapter.

Summary

Once you understand their core competencies, the artistry of complementing and not cloning lies in working with your customers, employees, and suppliers to eliminate redundant functions in the order fulfillment cycle. By complementing one another, you will enhance your combined strengths, and reduce your combined expenses. And most importantly, your company's EBIT, EBT, ROE, and ROI should improve dramatically.

Proactive Selling for Profitable Growth

Growth:
The Right Size
Company

Has your company lost customers, employees, orders, and suppliers to your competitors on a regular basis for an extended period of time? Have the results of these losses caused your company's EBIT, GP, and sales to decrease? Have you become a reactive manager, spending most of your time working on how to save customers, employees, orders, and suppliers rather than proactively growing your company? If this sounds all too familiar, your company may be the wrong size for its industry and market.

One of the most complex, difficult, and important accomplishments you can achieve as a manager is finding a balance in size between your company and its industry or market. It requires the artistry of a master chef preparing a wonderful meal, a highly gifted architect designing a great structure, or the masterful way some loving parents raise their children so that they become happy, healthy, and well-adjusted adults. There is a right size for most things, situations, and businesses, but there are no single simple right answers.

Before you can decide how much you want your company to grow, determine what is the right size for its industry and market. The process of answering the following questions you will enable to make a more informed decision. To accurately answer these questions about your company takes time and talent. You and key employees should be involved in the process.

To explain how the process works, I have provided answers for three hypothetical companies. Later in this chapter I discuss some of these companies' possible options. As with the hypothetical example I used in chapter seven, these examples are based on numerous real world experiences. Since each company is unique, it is the process that is more important, rather than what one company's manager decided was the right size for his or her company. My goal for this chapter is to explain the process in such a way that you can determine what is the right size for your company, if you have not already made that decision. The following are the hypothetical companies, followed by the list of questions, and answers for each of the companies.

A. A small privately owned single location distributor with no long-term debt.
B. A medium-sized privately owned regional distributor with no long-term debt.
C. A large publicly owned manufacturer with no long-term debt.

1. What is the SAM (served available market) for your company's goods and services?
   a) $100 million
   b) $2 billion
   c) $5 billion
2. What is your company's market share?
   a) 35 %
   b) 20 %
   c) 10 %
3. What is your company's market ranking, i.e. 1, 7, 9, 33, etc.?
   a) 1
   b) 2
   c) 3
4. What percent is your company's market growing per year?
   a) 20 %
   b) 20 %
   c) 15 %
5. From an EBITDA and existing lines of credit standpoint, how much can your company grow per year?
   a) 15 %

b) 10 %

c) 20 %

6. How much can your company grow per year without negatively impacting its EBIT?

a) 5 %

b) 10 %

c) 20 %

7. From a standpoint of control, how much can your company grow per year? That is, is the infrastructure in place to support the growth? If not, how long will it take to get it in place?

a) 25 %

b) 35 %

c) 10 % and one year of preparation to support the growth.

8. What positive leverage will your company gain from the growth in item 5 above (i.e., more and better customers and suppliers, a higher common stock selling price, the ability to attract better employees, etc.)?

a) There is none.

b) There is none.

c) We will have better (more profitable) customers.

9. What are the downside risks if your company doesn't grow?

a) The loss of major customers, major suppliers, and key employees.

b) The loss of major customers, major suppliers, and key employees.

c) Missing an opportunity to improve the company's earnings per share (EPS) and ROE.

10. How much can your company grow before you should be replaced as manager?

a) 50 %

b) 500 %

c) 300 %

What do all of these answers mean in terms of being the right size? These answer provide various options for each company, some of which follow:

Company A

Summarized background: Company A is a privately owned, small, single-location distributor with a 35 percent market share in a $100 million market and annual sales of $35 million. It is the largest distributor in a market that is growing at a rate of 20 percent per year. From an EBIDTA standpoint, the company can grow at a rate of 15 percent, or only 75 percent of the market's growth rate. Therefore, additional cash is required to maintain market share. However, with the company's present infrastructure, it can grow only 5 percent annually without negatively impacting the EBIT, even though it can remain under control with annual growth of 25 percent. There is no positive leverage that can be realized from the growth, but there is the risk of losing major customers, suppliers, and key employees. The owner/manager believes he or she can grow the company 50 percent before being replaced.

Possible options: Hire a manager; restructure the debt and infrastructure to support the market share growth and expansion into new markets; and design, plan, and sell new products. Or sell the company. What would you do if this were your company?

Company B

Summarized background: Company B is a privately owned, medium-sized regional distributor with a 20 percent market share in a $2 billion market and annual sales of $400,000. It is the second largest distributor in the marketplace and is growing at a rate of 20 percent per year. From an EBITDA standpoint, the company can grow at a rate of 10 percent, or only 50 percent of the market's growth rate. Therefore, additional cash is required to maintain market share. However, with the company's present infrastructure, it can only grow 10 percent annually without negatively impacting the EBIT, even though it can remain under control with annual growth of 35 percent. There is no positive leverage that can be realized from the growth, but there is the downside risk of losing major customers, suppliers, and key employees. The owner/manager believes he or she can grow the company 500 percent before being replaced.

Possible options: Restructure the debt and infrastructure for internal growth or expansion through acquisition within the current market, or in new markets. With a 20 percent market share that can be increased by 10 percent without negatively impacting the EBIT, there is an opportunity for existing market share growth. Also, since the owner/manger believes he or she can grow the business by 500 percent before he or she should be replaced, then an aggressive growth plan into new markets is probably appropriate. Or sell the company. What would you do?

Company C

Summarized background: Company C is a publicly owned, larger manufacturer with a 10 percent market share in a $5 billion market, with $500 million in annual sales. It is the third largest manufacturer in the market that is growing at a rate of 15 percent per year. From an EDITDA standpoint, the company can grow at a rate of 20 percent, or 33 percent faster than the market is growing. With the company's present infrastructure, it can grow 20 percent annually without negatively impacting the EBIT. There is the positive leverage of adding better (more profitable) customers as a direct result of being a larger manufacturer. If the company doesn't grow, it may miss an opportunity to increase EPS and ROE. The CEO of the company believes he or she can grow the company by 300 percent before being replaced.

Possible options: Grow with the available lines of credit, as the EBITDA can support growth of 20 percent annually. Aggressively attempt to become the largest company in the market. Becoming a larger company has a good upside potential, and as a public company, EPS growth should increase the stock's selling price. However, it will take one year to prepare the infrastructure to support the growth, so proper designing, planning, and implementation are required. Also, the CEO believes he or she is capable of growing the company by 300 percent per year before being replaced. Or he or she could recommend selling the company. If you were the CEO of this company, what would you suggest to the board?

As you may have noticed, with all three companies I suggested selling the company as a possible option. This is because the board and senior management of companies have a responsibility to maximize shareholder's value. Most companies have a selling price level that, if received, is the best known way at a given point in time to maximize the return to the company's shareholders.

The importance of and potential impact on a company being the right size for the business and market is significant. When your company is the right size, achieving your goals can be disproportionately easy. However, when your company is the wrong size, you can feel that every business day is an uphill battle experienced as if you were wearing hundred-pound shoes.

Let's examine a couple of industries that are familiar to most of us. If your company is an automobile manufacturer, it's probably better to be a large company, like one of the Big Three, or a small, niche automaker of specialty cars. Both the large and small types of automakers can be controlled profitable growth companies. Today, what may be the most difficult is to be a medium-sized automaker. One by one, most of the medium-sized companies have been acquired by, or are merging with, one of the industry's giants—or they're out of business.

Today, the same size dynamic applies to computer application (order fulfillment cycle) software companies. Many big and small niche application companies are thriving, while many medium-sized companies with generalized packages are struggling to survive. As in the automotive industry, many of the medium-sized companies have been acquired or had to merge with their competitors. When surviving means being bigger, industries evolve into consolidation modes.

Generally, the more a product or service is a commodity, the easier, faster, and more likely the industry will be dominated by a few large companies. Conversely, when a product or service is special and unique, the industry consolidation will be slower. In either case, industry consolidations are a fact of business life. As soon as possible you should decide what is the right size for your company. Again, there is no single answer that is appropriate for every company.

Summary

The artistry of managing the right size process lies in determining the size and attributes of your company, and then deciding how quickly you can achieve that size in a controlled profitable growth manner. Companies are like people—they come in all shapes, sizes, colors, and all levels of creativity, intelligence, health, wealth, and so forth.

If your company is not the right size for its industry, it can be negatively impacted in numerous ways. You can lose customers if they decide to purchase from national distributors and you are a single-location distributor. If you manage a small manufacturing company, the large contracts may go to the bigger companies because they have more financial strength. This can occur even though your company is more technically competent. When your company is too large or highly centralized, you may lose touch with your customers, which usually leads to losing them. Understand that there is no single "right" business model for every company, then be creative and consider using the Design, Plan, Make, Measure, and Analyze Process to make your company the right size—right now!

The Perfect
Customer

CHAPTER SEVENTEEN

You may think there's no such thing as the perfect customer. Well, you're right, and you're wrong. Here's why.

Several years ago Bill Erdmann, a seasoned and top-performing general manager of a contract manufacturing division, asked for my help. Bill is one of the best people with whom I've ever had the pleasure to work. His precision metal stamping division had a major problem. They were losing several customers whose products accounted for approximately 90 percent of sales and EBIT. The division made the same precision stamped metal part for all of the customers involved. The part's dimensional tolerances changed, becoming less precise. This made it possible for the part to be manufactured from plastic or by ultra-high volume metal stamping equipment, and this made Bill's division non-competitive.

Bill and his salespeople reviewed their options and were stuck. This was not because they weren't smart and didn't know their business. They were victims of previous successes and unable to resolve this problem. The division had been successful for so many years, the salespeople had forgotten how to generate significant new business. What they required was a fresh perspective and solution to their problem.

I invited Bill and his salespeople to a one-day offsite meeting. The controller was also invited to provide the financial information. I prepared an agenda for the meeting with two items:

1. What must we do to continue controlled profitable growth at our division?

2. What are the attributes of our division's perfect customer?

For this type of session, I've found taking employees away from their usual working environment generates better results. Because of the new surroundings with no interruptions, the employees are usually more creative. I prefer to have meetings like this in a conference room with a round table. The employees are positioned equally around the table, with no one at the head of the table. The room should have an easel with large sheets of paper and a board for writing and drawing. I structure the meeting as follows:

1. Ask the employees what they want to achieve at the meeting and write their responses where they're highly visible (15 to 30 minutes).

2. Hold an open discussion about what's required to continue controlled profitable growth at the division (3 hours).

3. Lunch, preferably offsite (1 hour and 30 minutes).

4. List the attributes of the division's perfect customer (15 to 30 minutes).

5. Hold an open discussion about the attributes of the division's perfect customer (1 hour).

6. Review the division's customers in relation to the attributes of the division's perfect customer (see the example in next section) (2 hours).

7. Develop a list of action items, including the date and place for the next meeting where the results will be reviewed (15 to 30 minutes).

After welcoming everyone, I asked the employees for their answers to the two agenda items. Then I wrote each employee's responses on a sheet of paper and affixed it to a wall. Some employees had one item, while others had several items they wanted to discuss.

The open discussion portion of the meeting resulted in a unanimous decision that new customers were needed. But what types of new customers? To answer this, the discussions changed to the attributes of their perfect customer. The following are the traits that make doing business with them profitable for the supplier company:

1. They are an industry leader.
2. They have and value long-term relationships with their customers, employees, and suppliers.
3. They believe in making and allowing their suppliers to make a fair profit.
4. They are financially strong.
5. Their products have an average life cycle of five years.
6. They adhere to the principles of TQM.
7. They are fair and honest and possess high business ethics.
8. They do business via e-commerce.
9. Their parts can be manufactured on 75 percent of the division's equipment.
10. They have an accurate ERP, MRP, MRP II system that minimizes rescheduling.

It is recommended that these attributes be rated in terms of value, with a 10 being the most important. Then rate your company's customers on a 0 to 10 basis, with 10 being the best score. Next, multiply the "value" times their "score." The following is an example of a format for rating customers:

CUSTOMERS

Attributes	Value x Score	A	B	C	D	E	F	G	H
1.									
2.									
3.									
4.									
5.									
6.									
7.									
8.									
9.									
10.									
Customer's Scores		—	—	—	—	—	—	—	—

This analysis allows you and your employees to determine which customers should generate higher EBIT and ROIs for your company. Bill's division had only two customers with approximately 80 percent of their perfect customer's attributes. Unfortunately, both customers were in the bottom 10 percent of the division's sales. Fortunately, this meant there was a large opportunity with both customers. Also, it was painfully clear the division needed a lot more new customers who matched their perfect customer's profile.

Next, determine what action items are required to maximize your company's results from this newly developed perfect customer profile. For Bill's division, this meant what must the employees do to increase sales with the two customers whose scores were eight hundred and what must they do to attract now customers?

When you develop Action Item Lists, always identify a specific person who is responsible for each item. Also, every action item must have a due date for completion. I've used the following format for the past two decades. It's simple, easy to use, and it works:

Person(s)   Item #(s)   Description(s)   Due Date(s)

This sequence makes it easy to review each person's Action Items individually, without the other people having to wait until their items are reviewed. Therefore, this approach saves time.

When the meeting for Bill's division ended, the employees began to implement the action items. Bill worked with his salespeople to develop their sales plans. When the plans were in place, the division's employees generated some remarkable results. For the next decade the division had excellent EBIT, ROI, and sales growth. Their highest-rated perfect customer was Hewlett-Packard's (HP) printer divisions. Managing a company can be very rewarding and a lot of fun when you have a world-class company like HP for a customer. Additionally, having the benefit of good timing really helped, because this one-day meeting occurred when HP entered the personal computer printer market.

As you can see from this anecdote about Bill's division, the definition of the perfect customer is the definition for a company's target customer as well. Therefore, an action item for every salesperson is to prepare a sales plan based on the perfect customer's profile. These sales plans should be prepared annually. I don't believe in voluminous sales plans. But I do believe in having appropriate and cost-effective sales plans. Have your salespeople use simple formats that include one page for each customer and a one-page salesperson's summary. The sales manager should prepare a one-page company sales plan summary that includes all the salespeople's plans.

When you review the sales plan format in chapter twenty-one, you'll notice it looks like a software's customer master and because it does, your company's software probably has the necessary fields for this information. Since sales plans are used for increasing sales, make the information available to your salespeople. Your salespeople need to know how they are performing in relation to their sales plans. Each salesperson's results should be reviewed by your sales manager on a quarterly and annual basis. When a salesperson has great results, thank him or her. Then share the information about the successful results with others. When a salesperson has poor performance, have your sales manager determine what caused the poor results. Then determine what you and your sales manager can do to help make this salesperson successful. When the problem is a lack of training and the salesperson is trainable, train him or her until he or she is successful.

Long-term profitability is good and necessary to support a company's growth. This requires selling to customers who contribute to the company's EBIT. Unfortunately, sometimes companies have unprofitable customers. And most companies can't afford unprofitable business for any extended period of time. Companies can and do have unprofitable customer orders. This may occur for strategic business reasons. But that's very different from all of a customer's business being unprofitable. If your company has unprofitable customers, and you've tried unsuccessfully to improve the profitability, then it's time to end that business relationship. I know how hard it is to get new customers and to lose existing ones. However, sometimes it's the only viable option. When this happens, always end the relationship in a gracious way, as if no one is to blame. The relationship wasn't complementary. Everyone tried, but it just didn't work out, so it's time to move on.

Earlier I wrote about one of my mentors, Manny Krupin. As you may recall, during my truck driver days Manny wanted me to visit him every time I made a delivery to his division. On one such visit he gave me some golden information regarding customers. To paraphrase, here's what Manny said: "Paul, no matter what anyone else tells you, remember it's better to have ten customers at $1,000 per month in sales with a 30 percent GP, than it is to have one customer at $10,000 a month in sales with a 20 percent GP." Do you know why? Because you don't want to have all your eggs in one basket, and the role of a distributor is to sell and service the smaller customers. You make a higher GP and, all things being equal, should make a better EBIT and ROI as well. Manny's division made a lot of money doing business with his perfect customers.

Summary

The artistry of managing the perfect customer process lies in defining, and then finding the customers who value and pay for your company's products and services. Focusing your company's resources on the perfect customers can dramatically improve the company's ROE, ROI, EBIT, and sales growth. You and your employees should develop long-term, in-depth relationships with the employees of the perfect customers. To a large extent they are, and will be, responsible for your company's present and future successes. Again, *people*, whether customers, employees, or suppliers, are our business.

The Perfect Supplier Partner

Partnering is a relationship that can exist between a company and its customers and suppliers. Partnering may or may not be contractual. Successful partnering is the win-win relationship between people and companies. An important goal of successful partnering is achieved when the parties involved complement but don't clone the core competencies of the other.

The difference between the perfect supplier and the perfect customer is in the evaluation process. Both parties, customer and supplier, evaluate one another. To start a basic partnering relationship with a supplier, perform the following five steps:

1. Develop a list of the attributes of the perfect supplier per the process described in chapter seventeen for the perfect customer.

2. Evaluate the suppliers who represent 80 percent (applying Pareto's Law again) of your company's annual purchases. Base this evaluation on the attributes of the perfect supplier.

3. Meet with the management of the supplier companies who are in your company's top 80 percent of annual purchases. Explain the perfect supplier process. Then ask them if they are interested in developing a perfect partnering relationship with your company. When they are interested, have them complete step 1 above. Next, establish a date, time, and place to review their views of you and your company, per item 1. By compar-

ing these results in a joint meeting, both company's employees can determine if they value the same attributes.

4. When both company's management agree to proceed, develop an Action Item List (see chapter seventeen for the format) for all mutually beneficial attributes. The Action Item List should have one employee from each company responsible for each item, and a due date for completion. Also, establish a date, time, and place for the next meeting where both company's employees will review the results from the Action Item List.

5. The Action Item List is the perfect customer/supplier plan for both companies. Measure all the items from the first day they are implemented. A successful perfect partnering program is one where the companies, employees, management, and shareholders make more money for their time or higher ROI, while improving customer satisfaction. If this is not the case, don't give up on partnering! Instead, go back to step 1 and start the perfect supplier process over again. What you and your employees learned from their first attempt can be used to make the second experience successful.

There is an old saying that none of us is as smart as all of us. This is really the essence of the perfect supplier, and partnering in general. No person or company has the resources to do everything. Also, we don't have the time to convince every customer and supplier about the importance of partnering. Since we all have finite resources, we should partner with companies that allow our companies to earn the most EBIT, ROE, and ROI.

Partnering can be as informal as a verbal understanding between two people, or as formal as a very lengthy and complex legal document between people and companies. Effective partnering occurs when the expectations of the parties involved are met or exceeded. An example of one form of partnering is the customers' certified supplier programs. Customers establish criteria for suppliers to become certified (approved). In exchange for the suppliers becoming certified, they are allowed to quote on the customers' requirements that are within their capabilities. Frequently these partnering agreements lead to the customers dealing with fewer suppliers and the suppliers having fewer customers. This focus and interdependence for financial success are the driving forces for partnering.

I use the terms "perfect supplier" and "perfect customer" to reinforce the importance of doing business with the companies that complement your company. These are the customers and suppliers who want a win-win, long-term profitable growth relationship with your company.

As I'm writing this chapter, I am also preparing for a panel discussion on partnering with suppliers. I am this session's moderator for PrintImage International's Mid-Winter 1999 Conference. PrintImage International is an industry association for the quick (instant, pay-for-print) printers. This association's members, along with most of the organization's members I've been involved with, know the importance of partnering.

Summary

The artistry of managing the perfect supplier process comes with aligning your company with the best customers and suppliers. Perfect suppliers are the companies that allow your company to earn the most amount of EBIT, ROE, and ROI. Focus on these customers and suppliers, because they are essential to your company's long-term profitable growth.

Good Salespeople Sell
and Relationship Selling

After having dealt with thousands of salespeople, I believe: Good salespeople sell. Good salespeople develop long-term relationships with their customers, fellow employees, management, and suppliers. They know that a large portion of their success is the result of good relationships. My beliefs about salespeople began after I was a general manager for five years.

My sales manager Carl Hofmann and I interviewed and hired all the company's salespeople. We also had other supervisors involved in the interviewing process. This made it very expensive to interview and add a new salesperson. But, we wanted the best available salespeople, so I viewed this as a wise investment. Some of the salespeople we hired were very successful, others had moderate successes, and some were unsuccessful. After discovering our hiring success rate was only 50 percent, Carl and I had a series of long and introspective conversations. We had been so careful and thorough in our interviewing process that we found it difficult to believe only 50 percent of the people we hired became successful. Therefore, we knew we must change and improve the interviewing process.

During the following two months, we reviewed every salesperson's results for the previous five years. From this research we learned that good salespeople sell. So what traits made a sales candidate successful in our company? What we discovered was the successful salespeople had certain key characteristics in common.

157

The successful salespeople who worked for our company had most of the following ten characteristics:

1. They had a history of successful selling, as measured by themselves and the companies for whom they worked.
2. They wanted to earn enough money to exceed their financial needs and the expectations of the company's management. Also, it was important for them to be viewed by their peers as being very successful "winners."
3. They did not want any cap (limit) on their income.
4. They were likable and truly enjoyed people. Most importantly, they knew how to build and maintain good long-term relationships.
5. They had a history of successfully selling products or services where the order fulfillment cycle time was similar to our company's.
6. They were honest and had above-average intelligence, although not necessarily having earned a college degree.
7. They convinced the employees who supported them about the importance of their customers to the overall success of the company.
8. They had above-average business knowledge, and most importantly, knew what was required to make a profit.
9. They viewed every customer's order as their order. Also, customer satisfaction was their responsibility.
10. They had excellent work ethics and were available for business issues on a twenty-four-hour-a-day, seven-day-a-week basis (24x7).

The dominant characteristic all the successful salespeople had in common was their ability to sell, no matter what! By reviewing a salesperson's results, and only their results, it was by far the best indicator of future successes. Good salespeople sell. Carl's way of expressing this was by using the term POIF, meaning "purchase-order-in-fist." In other words, where's the (customer's) order?

I know this may seem obvious, but sometimes a salesperson's style can cause managers to overlook their results. Also, salespeople do know how to sell, and sometimes their target customer is their manager. When a salesperson is spending more time selling to you than selling to your customers, you have a problem.

After Carl and I had our realization, we took a different approach to our interviewing. We found that when a sales candidate wasn't a "job hopper" (working two years or less for several companies) and had approximately eight of the ten traits listed above, he or she would be successful in the company. Having industry knowledge was important for some salespeople. However, it was not the main factor in determining a salesperson's success or failure. For some salespeople, having industry knowledge was actually a hindrance because their experiences limited their ability to think of "out-of-the-box" solutions. Also, they may have acquired industry-related bad work habits along the way. Conversely, a salesperson without industry knowledge didn't know what was possible—or impossible. Sometimes, when the industry knowledgeable salesperson saw obstacles, the salesperson without industry knowledge saw opportunities. Because of this learning experience, for the next three years our "batting average" went from .500 to .800, as salespeople were selected who became successful 80 percent of the time.

The best salesperson I have ever hired had no industry experience at all. I ran an ad in Sunday's newspaper for a salesperson. The ad stated the company had an excellent career opportunity for an electronic sub-system salesperson. I received the best resumes for a sales position from this ad I had ever seen. Carl and I went through our normal process of reviewing each resume, then called the candidates we both believed could do a good job for the company. The day after the ad ran, I received a call from a salesperson who was at an airport in between flights. He had taken the Sunday paper with him, seen our ad, and wanted to talk with me. He didn't have a resume or any industry experience. During our brief conversation, he partially sold me on his abilities to sell. This is in part due to the questions he asked. He wanted to know the following about the opportunity:

1. Was there any limit on the amount he could make?
2. How long did I think it would take for him to learn the technical side of the business?
3. Why did I believe this was a good opportunity?
4. How soon could we meet so he could show me face-to-face why he is a successful salesman?

On my desk was a stack of great resumes for this sales position. Why did I need to talk to this guy with no resume and no industry experience? Because his questions caught my interest, and he was "reading" me as the conversation continued. I believed he might be that special kind of salesperson who is a natural at what he does and will be successful—no matter what!

By design, we interviewed this candidate last. As I expected, the interview went well. During the interviewing he continued to ask astute questions and give intelligent answers. After the interview, Carl and I agreed we had a potential superstar in this candidate. We then had him meet with the operations manager and office manager. When all the interviews concluded, we met in my office and agreed this was a person we wanted to work with and have represent our company. The following day we hired him.

He started approximately two weeks after that. In five months his commission exceeded his draw. At the end of his second year with the company he had increased his sales by 400 percent and became the top-performing salesperson in the company. When Carl retired, he became the sales manager. He had all of the good salesperson's traits discussed in this chapter. He was a real winner!

So where can you find salespeople who will become the "real winners" for your company? Sometimes they are found in non-traditional places. Some time ago, one of my best general managers, Susan Thuet, had a problem finding good salespeople. Her division was located in the center of Silicon Valley where the demand for qualified, technical sales professionals was very high. For several months she tried to find a good entry-level person she could hire and train. Susan was an excellent, creative salesperson, with a high level of people savvy. One day over lunch we did some brainstorming and came up with a new approach for finding salespeople in a high-demand employment market.

Our discussion focused on what we believed were the most important non-technical aspects of being a good salesperson. The more we brainstormed, the more we kept coming back to the same conclusion—the person had to be likable and bright, with good people savvy. We then discussed what she would do to find someone.

The next person Susan met who was likable, bright and had good people savvy would be offered an interview for an entry-level technical sales position. As it turned out, the next person was a waiter. After several in-depth discussions with the waiter, Susan made him an offer, which he accepted. He started two weeks later. After six months, he was the second highest sales producer in the division. It takes courage, creativity, and a commitment to training when you hire a non-technical person for a technical sales position.

Good salespeople have high Hit Rates. As a refresher, the Hit Rate measures the percentage of customer RFQs that become customer orders. When a salesperson brings in twenty RFQs during the month and sixteen become customer orders, the salesperson has an 80 percent Hit Rate (16 ÷ 20 = 80 %). Every purchase order from a customer starts with an RFQ. Every RFQ, no matter how simple, has a preparation cost to your company. Therefore, it is very important to track (see pages 66-67 and 184) each salesperson's Hit Rate.

I've found the best salespeople average around an 80 percent Hit Rate, not 100 percent. This is because with 100 percent, the salesperson is receiving RFQs for repeat business. This approach does not allow you to see what new products and services are being asked for by your customers. You require salespeople who generate a certain percentage of opportunities that are beyond your company's present capabilities. This is one of the best ways for you to keep informed about your customer's current wants and needs.

Another valuable characteristic of most top-performing salespeople is what I call "The Sherlock Holmes Trait." This means having a "nose" for investigating and finding the real opportunities. The traditional business term to partially describe this trait is "marketing," but it is really more than that. This trait includes an intuitive sense for where the "live ones" (real opportunities) exist. Every successful salesperson I have worked with spent approximately 20 percent of his or her time doing Sherlock Holmes work. They designed and planned their sales strategies before making any sales calls. As I discussed in chapter seven, the Design, Plan, Make, Measure, and Analyze Process can make every company, job, and project more successful. This is especially true for salespeople.

Some managers are big believers in aptitude testing for all candidates. They further believe that no matter how strong the candidate's track record is, he or she must pass the test to be hired. I believe candidate testing is generally accurate but may be specifically inaccurate. When a large enough population is tested, the results are generally accurate. The obvious exceptions to my belief is any kind of testing for a specific skill or discipline. This would be the testing or certification of accountants, attorneys, engineers, doctors, and so forth. But for the testing of one sales candidate, I found using the ten-item criteria listed above to be a better predictor of a salesperson's future success or failure.

Managers really require two main results from their salespeople:

1. To generate RFQs from customers that become profitable orders.
2. To develop excellent long-term relationships with their customers.

In my experience, the sales professionals who are the best at accomplishing this don't like to be managed with a short leash. The top performers have a combination of many skills and traits. Over-managing them usually generates lower sales and frustrates everyone in the process. As the manager, focus on the salesperson's results not on their style.

Salespeople function as your company's eyes, ears, and mouths. They have more contact with customers than anyone else in your company. They are the "rocket ship" that when properly managed will successfully take your company into the future. As strongly as I believe people are our business, good salespeople are our company's investment in the future.

Summary

The artistry of managing relationship selling is first understanding that good salespeople sell. This is for several reasons: Good salespeople develop excellent, multiple long-term business relationships with customers, fellow employees, and suppliers. These various relationships act as a company's insurance policy when a key contact leaves a company. As the manager, you too should have multiple, excellent long-term business relationships with customers, employees, and suppliers. As the manager you should focus on your salespeople's results, rather than on their styles. People are our business and having good business relationships is the name of the game.

Funneling

CHAPTER TWENTY

Have you ever used a funnel to pour liquid from one container into another? The funnel makes it possible for you to pour the liquid without spilling it. Yes, you do need the right size funnel, and yes, you can only pour the liquid at a certain rate so the funnel won't overflow. But without the funnel, you would be hard-pressed to find a better way to get all the liquid from one container to another. This analogy shows how funneling is used to get valuable information from your customers to your salespeople and you.

Funneling, as an information-gathering process, may be a new term for you. However, it is probably something you and your better salespeople do on a regular basis. A physical funnel is much more open at the top, and gradually narrows until reaching its spigot. This is exactly how the questioning portion of the funneling process flows. You start by asking the person you want to get information from big open-ended questions (questions that can't be answered with a yes, no, or single piece of information). Then ask progressively narrower questions along with a few closed-ended questions (questions that can be answered with a yes, no, or single piece of information.)

An example of an open-ended question your salesperson might ask a buyer is: What are the biggest purchasing problems facing your company? Since the respondent can't answer this question with a yes, no, or single piece of information, their answer contains information they decided was the appropriate response. Therefore, this answer may contain, or lead to, more valuable information. Also, it can be about a topic your salesperson could not have known about. After the buyer answers your salesperson's first open-ended question, a slightly narrower open-ended question should be asked. The next question could be: How do these problems impact your job? A closed-ended question your salesperson might ask is: How many dollars of raw material does your company purchase a year? There is no specific number of questions to ask, as every situation is different. What's important is to ask enough questions and get enough answers so new opportunities can be generated for your company. Therefore, the goal of the first phase of the funneling process is to receive an informal or formal RFQ.

Your sales manager should meet with the salesperson immediately after the customer interview. Then the two of them should review the information and determine if an opportunity exists for your company. Categorize the customer's responses in three ways:

1. The company offers products and services to meet this customer's requirements.

2. The company will offer products and services to meet this customer's requirements.

3. It is highly unlikely that the company will provide these products and services in the foreseeable future.

Next, use the information gathered from the customer, along with the company's capabilities, to develop a proposal. Visually, the proposal portion of the process is turning the funnel upside down. Functionally, this is the opposite flow used to gather the information, as it is from specific to general. The sales manager and salesperson should develop a proposal and response for the customer. First, develop a proposal for the customer's requirements that are within your company's existing products and services. Then develop a response to the customer's requirements your company will be able to provide in the near future. Next, "no bid" (do not quote on) those customer requirements your company will not be able to provide. All of this information should be contained in one document, that can be used as a talking paper and written proposal.

It is important to remember that the customer may not have a current RFQ for your company's products and services. This is fine, because the proposal can be used to address solutions for future

RFQs. The goal is to get your company's name on the Approved Vendor Listing (AVL) for these products and services. If there is an actual RFQ when your company's proposal is made, great. Just don't expect it. Your goal is to position your company for future opportunities.

Sometimes when a company no bids a portion of an RFQ or proposal, it causes the company to lose the entire opportunity. Therefore, when your sales manager, salespeople, or you recall that other customers recently requested these same products and services your company has no bid, you should immediately meet. Your involvement is required because these discussions may conclude that new products, services, and capital expenditures are required. If you and your employees really believe in customer satisfaction, these customer-requested products and services must be thoroughly investigated.

This is not to say your company should provide all things to every customer. However, when several customers are asking for the same thing, you don't want to miss an opportunity. A prime example of this is when the American automobile industry missed the initial economical small car opportunity several decades ago. Eventually they realized their mistake, but then they had to catch up to the rest of the market. Frequently, these new capabilities are inexpensive and/or suitable for outsourcing. When this is the case, why not provide them now?

An analogy from the children's story about Johnny Appleseed should help you remember the funneling process. As you may recall, Johnny traveled back and forth across the United States looking for suitable places to plant his apple seeds. After selecting the right places (customers) to plant his apple seeds, he watered the seeds until they turned into trees (RFQs). Then he nourished the trees until they bore beautiful apples (customer purchase orders). The part of Johnny's process that involved carefully selecting the right places (customers) to plant his apple seeds is what top-performing salespeople do in selecting the right customers for the funneling process.

It may take some of your salespeople a while to understand and use funneling. When this occurs, try teaching them by using role-playing exercises. Start with you or your sales manager being the buyer. Teach your salespeople how and when to use open-ended and closed-ended questions. When they grasp the concepts, reverse the roles and start the funneling process over again.

When you, your sales manager, and salesperson are comfortable with the salesperson's newly acquired knowledge, have your sales manager make a joint sales call with the salesperson. This is done to determine how well the salesperson uses funneling in a real-world situation. If necessary, remind your sales manager to critique the salesperson *after* meeting with the customer. This may seem very obvious, but some sales managers want to show their customers and their salespeople how smart they are. Obviously, this is inappropriate and can retard the learning process. If the salesperson is able to use the funneling process, great—on to the next salesperson. When they can't, it's time for more role playing or another teaching technique.

Summary

The artistry of managing the funneling process lies in its utility as a powerful tool that increases your company's sales. It is based on asking appropriate open and closed-ended questions. Then, after listening intently to the answers, developing proposals to generate RFQs that become customer orders. The process takes time to develop, so this is a situation where patience really is a virtue.

Sales Management and a Sales Management System

My number one mentor, Nate Landgarten (whom I wrote about in the acknowledgment section of this book), has a saying that he's repeated thousands of times: "If a company doesn't grow, it will die." I also believe this to be true, and it is one of the reasons why proper sales management is so important to the success and survival of every company.

When you are the manager of a small to medium size company, you may also function as the company's sales manager. For most managers with more than five or six salespeople, and total direct reports of ten or more, I've found a sales manager or vice president of sales is required. The sales manager's job is to design, plan, make, measure, and analyze a company's sales. A company's management requires a sales management system that is results-oriented. I've seen, developed, and worked with many sales management systems. Some were complicated, time-consuming, and rarely used. Others were so limited, they were equally useless.

A well-designed sales management system includes the information required to satisfy the company's management, customers, employees, and suppliers. All four groups have one thing in common. They all want results. The company's management and suppliers want GP, market share, and sales growth. The customers want the lowest total cost of procurement. The employees want to maximize their incomes. The artistry in designing and implementing a sales management system is in satisfying the requirements of all four groups, with one system. The following is an example of a simple, yet effective, sales management system.

Before the end of company's business year, have your sales manager and each salesperson prepare an annual sales plan. These plans describe what your sales manager and salespeople want to accomplish during the following year. There should be a one-page annual sales plan for each customer and a one-page sales plan summary for each salesperson. This summary should include every salesperson's customers.

The sales manager should prepare the company's annual sales plan summary. This plan should have a one-page summary for all the salespeople, with grand totals included. Also, when your sales manager has his or her own customers, he or she should complete a salesperson's sales plan as well. No matter how big your company is, your sales manager should have some direct customer responsibility. This is to ensure he or she never forgets what is required to be a salesperson.

All the annual sales plans should include sales, GP dollars, and percents. There should be monthly, quarterly, and year-to-date subtotals and totals. Also, there should be fields for the percent and dollar changes, from one period to another, and from the same period's prior year's results. The one-page annual sales plan for each customer requires the following information:

1. Customer name
2. Customer address(s)
3. Customer telephone number(s)
4. Customer e-mail address(s)
5. Customer Web site address
6. SIC code(s)
7. Primary industry
8. Secondary industries
9. Company Chairman
10. Company CEO
11. Company President
12. Company COO

13. Company CFO

14. Buyer(s)

15. Customer annual sales

16. Credit rating

17. The customer's annual SAM purchases (the customer's annual purchases of the products, served available market the company can supply)

18. The company's prior year's sales to the customer as a percentage of the customer's total annual purchases

19. The company's prior year's sales and GP dollars and percentage to the customer

20. Current year's annualized sales and GP dollars and percentage to the customer

21. GP dollars per product and per shipment on sales to the customer; by quarter, year-to-date, annual, and prior year

22. Current year's annualized sales as a percentage of the customer's total annual purchases

23. Current year's sales goal by quarter for the customer

24. Current year's annualized sales as a percentage of the sales goal

25. Products sold to the customer during the previous twelve months by supplier, with descriptions and part numbers

26. The new parts, products, and services the salesperson plans to sell to the customer next year

27. The plans for how these new parts, products, and services will be sold to the customer

28. The additional resources required to meet or exceed the salesperson's plan

After you and your sales manager approve the sales plans, it's time to make it happen! It is the sales manager's direct responsibility to achieve the planned results. This can be accomplished in many ways. One of the most effective ways is to work with all your salespeople to help them achieve their goals. Every salesperson has his or her own areas that require improvement. Therefore, your sales manager should teach each salesperson the necessary skills to successfully meet or exceed their plans.

Each salesperson's annual sales plan must be reviewed by your sales manager on a quarterly basis. These reviews are to compare the planned results, to actual results. When there is a negative variance, a Gap Analysis must be done for all customers who are below the salesperson's plan. This analysis should be completed by the salesperson and approved by your sales manager in a maximum of one week. The corrective action plans generated from the Gap Analyses should be reviewed in one month and again at the quarterly session. This is to ensure that the new plans are actually working. When the plans aren't working, find out why and make the necessary changes.

Since your sales manager is responsible for your company's sales growth, when there are salespeople whose results are always below their plans and they have been thoroughly trained, they must be replaced by the sales manager. Ineffective salespeople are a company's most expensive employees. This is because when they are not achieving their sales plans, the company's growth is stunted. Lack of growth can force you to terminate good employees for lack of work. You and your other employees will make less money. Your company's shareholders will receive lower returns on their investments. The available funds for research and development will be reduced. I think you get the picture. Remember: Good salespeople sell, no matter what!.

When general managers who are responsible for profit centers report to you, I believe it is best to have them prepare summary forecast information. As managers, they probably have their own methods for developing annual sales plans and budgets. When they give you and the company the results they forecast, what is gained by insisting that they use your sales planning methodology? Good managers know what is appropriate for their divisions or profit centers. New managers, or managers who required additional training, are usually very open to accepting assistance with their planning and budgeting.

To keep it simple and effective, I ask managers to submit the following information to me for the next fiscal year two months before the end of the current fiscal year (this allows me time to review, comment, discuss, and sometimes negotiate with the managers about their plans):

1. Sales dollars
2. GP dollars
3. GP percent

4. ROI percent
5. Required capital expenditure(s): description(s) and dollars
6. Required people: description(s) and dollars
7. Top ten customers by dollar
8. Top ten suppliers by dollar

Initially, this information was supplied to me manually on one sheet of paper. Later, this was automated to a software spreadsheet, with quarterly categories, and submitted electronically.

Summary

The artistry of sales management begins with hiring the best salespeople. As soon as they're onboard, they should develop annual sales plans for each of their customers. Then lead, train, coach, and motivate them. Because, the profitable growth of your company depends to a large extent on them. Manage them based on their individual skills and talents. Don't use a "cookie cutter" approach on talented sales professionals, because their successful individual styles vary so widely. Remember, your company needs results not reports. Therefore, use a simple sales management system. Don't bog down your sales manager and salespeople with administrative work. They must spend as much of their prime time as possible with customers.

Epilogue

Do the
Right Thing

Up until now, I've written about techniques, methods, and business information that can make you a better manager. In turn, you will be able to improve the performance of your employees and company. These techniques and methods are the means to an end but not the end. Everything must be tempered by doing good actions as a citizen, employee, person, and manager. I believe it's important to use your knowledge, experiences, and resources to make the world a better place.

Inside most of us is the capacity to know the difference between right and wrong. When you believe in something but you know things aren't being done right, you must be willing to fight. This will not always put you in the politically correct or popular position. But when you believe you're right, stick by your beliefs, popular or not.

I've written this book because I wanted to share some of the best things I've learned about business. Did I make mistakes along the way? Absolutely! But I made a point of learning from them so I wouldn't make the same mistake twice. I hope some of the topics I've written about have given you new information and that you will make fewer mistakes than I did.

Managers and employees have various motives for doing what they do during their careers. While working, and long after your career is over, how do you want to be known and remembered? I don't know how you want to be remembered, because I don't know what is right for you. However, what I can share with you is that in my dealings with thousands of people during my lifetime, character, compassion, integrity, honesty, and loyalty do matter. Others around you may play the game by their own set of self-serving rules. Sometimes, they may even appear to be winning. But I've found that an old saying is still very true: "What goes around, comes around." Somewhere, sometime, somehow, these misguided individuals usually get what they deserve. We may not be there to witness it, but it happens just the same. All you can really do is be accountable for your own actions and *do the right thing.*

Summary

The artistry of doing the right thing is more than abiding by the law or following the company's handbook. Your life is more than what you do for work. Doing the right thing involves the totality of your dealings with people in all areas of your life. Therefore, doing the right thing involves being the best person you can be, in all that you do, every day. Listen to your inner self and follow your feelings about what's right for you, as long as it doesn't hurt others. Stick by your guns and be willing to fight for what you believe in. You will make a difference!

During his thirty plus years as an employee and manager, Paul F. Doucette has worked in just about every position that exists in the business world. He worked for a discount department store while he was attending junior college. While earning his BA degree at California State University, Northridge (CSUN), he began working for a diversified distribution and manufacturing NYSE company. He started his twenty-nine year career with this company as a temporary part-time truck driver, and advanced to corporate officer and executive vice president. He also worked as an inspector, quality assurance representative, outside salesperson, production control manager, operations manager, general manager, vice president, senior vice president, and president of a highly diversified $225 million business group. He has also held corporate responsibilities for quality, recruitment facilities, and telecommunications. His career at the division, business group, and corporate level is marked by outstanding results and accomplishments. Paul has worked with such companies as 3M, Agfa, Ampex, Creo, DuPont, Hewlett-Packard, Imation, Kodak, Konica, Mitsubishi, Motorola, National Semiconductor, Polaroid, SAP, Scitex, and Unisys. In 1998 he formed the Doucette Corporation to provide consultative strategic business services to senior management.

After receiving his MBA, he worked with Pepperdine University MBA students as a mentor to facilitate the "real world" portion of their learning experiences. From 1996 through 2000 he served as the secretary and treasurer for the North American Graphic Arts Suppliers Association (NAGASA), which represents the six billion dollar printing and publishing industry. In 1998 he became a member of the Board of Director's Human Resources Committee for Daniel Freeman and Santa Marta Hospitals. Recently he became a management consultant for the Executive Service Corps (ESC) of Southern California. ESC provides management consulting services to non-profit organizations. In the 1980s he was a board member of a community-based environmental group that stopped coastal oil drilling adjacent to Santa Monica Bay. He and his wife Daryl married in 1968. They live in the Pacific Palisades, a suburb of Los Angeles, California.

Action Item List: A list of specific tasks that includes the person(s), description(s), and due date(s) for all items required to complete a project.

Actual Costs: What a company actually paid for labor, material, services, and so forth.

Analysis Paralysis: Over-analyzing an opportunity, problem, or process, without making a decision as to the action that is required.

A/P: Accounts Payable. Debts a company must pay off within the year, that is, a current liability. Typically, these debts are to the company's suppliers.

Application Software: Software for the transaction processing of the order fulfillment cycle. The application software includes such modules as order entry, material management, accounts payable, logistics, credit and collection, and so forth.

A/R: Accounts Receivable. Money owed to a company by its customers; it qualifies as a current asset because the company expects the money to be paid to it within the year.

Average Annual Total Return: Often called the internal rate of return (IRR), the average annual total return is a percentage equal to the interest rate on a bank account that would give you the same total return on your investment. It takes into account money earned by the investment (interest, dividends, and capital gains distributions) as well as changes in share price. Since it is an annual rate, it acts like a bank interest rate that compounds annually.

Average Investment: The investment that is generally averaged on a quarterly, year-to-date, or annual basis.

AVL: Approved Vendor Listing. A list compiled by a company of approved vendors, suppliers, and materials. This approval is generally done by the quality, engineering, and financial departments of the company preparing the AVL.

Balance Sheet: An official financial statement that includes a company's assets (things it owns, such as cash, capital equipment, and investments) and liabilities (things it owes, such as accounts payable, long-term debt, and shareholder's equity). To determine a company's net worth, subtract its liabilities from the fair market value of its assets.

Benchmarking: An improvement process in which a company measures its performance against that of the best-in-class companies, determines how those companies achieved their performance levels, and uses the information to improve its performance. The subjects that can be benchmarked include strategies, operations, processes, and procedures.

Best-in-Class: Within a category of organizations, the best-performing entity, as compared to all of the peers.

Best Practices: The best way to perform a task or operation.

BOM: Bill of Material. A list of all the materials required to make a part number.

Book Value: The total recorded asset value of a company and total liabilities. Intangible assets include items such as goodwill and patents, which may have no historical cost and therefore are not recorded assets.

Branch: A company's location that generally performs only such limited functions as inside sales, outside sales, and customer service. Some companies have branches that also perform the distribution center functions.

Break-Even Point: The point at which a company's gross profit or gross margin is equal to its expenses.

Business Plan: A written proposal for a startup business, or a new business direction in a previously established business. Business plans typically include a description of the company and its products or services, a budget, an overview of the current and projected financing, a marketing strategy, and projected profits and losses.

C Corporation: A general corporation that is the most common type of corporation. There is no limit to the number of shareholders. Since the corporation is a separate entity, the personal assets of each shareholder are protected from creditors of the corporation. Therefore, the shareholder's liability is limited to the amount they invested in the corporation's stock.

Cap-X: Capital Expenditure. The money a company uses to purchase such assets as equipment, land, and buildings.

Cash Flow: A measurement of the money going into and coming out of a company. If a company has a negative cash flow, this means the company must borrow money, or look to investors for additional capital to operate its business. If a company has a positive cash flow, this means the company has money to spend on research and development, expanding operations, dividends to investors, and so on.

CD: Certificate of Deposit. An investment offered by banks that guarantees a specific rate of return for a specific term, and is FDIC insured.

Closed-Ended Question: A question that *can* be answered with a *yes*, *no*, or specific piece of information.

COGS: Cost of Goods Sold. This amount represents the cost of buying raw materials and producing the goods that a company sells. It also includes the cost of the company's labor force as well as its manufacturing burden and other expenses.

Contract Manufacturer: A Job Shop. A contract manufacturer makes parts, sub-assemblies, assemblies, or provides direct labor services to another company's specifications.

Control Chart: A chart that has upper and lower limits where values of some statistical measures for a series of parts are plotted. Frequently, it will have a center line to help indicate a trend of the plotted values toward either control limit.

Corporation: A legal entity formed by one or more persons. A corporation is formed under the laws of a specific state and is legally defined as having a separate existence from that of its founders or owners.

Corrective Action Plan: A plan with solutions to eliminate an identified problem.

Customer Class: Categorizing your customers based on the type, size, profitability, and so forth. The customer classes are used to segment your customers for the purpose of improving sales, profitability, and customer service.

Debt-to-Equity Ratio: The ratio of a company's long-term liabilities (those that won't be paid off in one year) to its equity (total value of stock). The higher the level of debt, the more important it is for a company to have positive earnings and steady cash flow. Debt in and of itself in not bad, but since it requires the timely payout of interest to debt holders, it is important to analyze a company within the context of the likelihood it will have adequate resources to meet its payments in the coming business and economic environment. By the nature of certain industries, you will find that some contain only companies with a high ratio (or vice-versa). For comparative purposes, debt-to-equity ratio is most useful for companies within the same industry.

Depreciation: A fixed asset's depreciable life is the commonly accepted period of time during which it is useful. Depreciation is an accounting procedure that spreads the asset's purchase cost over its depreciable life. For example, a fixed asset that costs $10,000 and lasts ten years could be depreciated by $1,000 a year for ten years. For accounting purposes, this reduces its book value by $1,000 each year, until at the end of its "useful life," it is worth nothing. Depreciation reduces net income but does not reduce cash.

Detailed Estimate: A listing of all the material, outside processing, direct labor, and tooling that is required to manufacture or assemble a part.

Direct Labor: The labor that a company uses in the manufacturing process.

Distribution Center: The warehouse portion of a company's logistics system.

Distributor(s): A company that doesn't manufacture the items it sells. The role of the distributor is to complement the manufacturers it represents. Generally, distributors sell, warehouse, and deliver products they have purchased from the manufacturers.

Division: A business unit that is part a parent company. Generally, a division performs most of the functions of a standalone business and is measured as a separate profit center.

DSO: (Number of Average) Day's Sales Outstanding. A company's annual sales divided by 365 equals the average day's sales.

EBIT: Earnings Before Interest and Taxes.

EBITDA: Earnings Before Interest Taxes Depreciation and Amortization. Or pretax cash flow.

EBT: Earnings Before Taxes.

E-Commerce: Electronic Commerce. Commerce without paper. A term that in its broadest definition includes business done via the Internet, computer to computer, remote device to computer, telephone to computer, and fax.

EPS: Earnings per Share. The amount of after-tax income a company earns divided by the number of shares of common stock.

Equity: Ownership. When you own part of something, you have equity in it. For example, when you own three thousand shares of Company XYZ's stock, that is your equity in the corporation. In other words, you and the other shareholders own a piece of the corporation.

ERP: Enterprise Resources Planning. Planning that involves every operation within a company's value chain in order to minimize the cost and time of getting products to customers.

Estimate Summary: The total costs of all the material, outside processing, direct labor, and tooling that is required to manufacture or assemble a part.

FASB: Financial Accounting Standards Board.

FIFO: First-In-First-Out: This is an accounting and costing method for a company's inventory. The cost of the oldest (first-in) unit on hand is used when establishing the inventory value at the time of a sale (first-out), and for valuing the inventory.

Fill Rate: Same as Service Level. The measurement of the effectiveness of a company's entire material management system. It is a measurement of standard items ordered in relation to the percentage that were filled completely at the time of order entry.

Fixed Assets: Fixed assets are tangible items used in the operation of a business but not consumed in the course of those operations. These are also known as "capital assets." Some examples of fixed assets are the company's buildings or machinery with which a product is made.

Fixed Costs: Costs that don't vary because of changes in activity. Examples include lease payments and long-term debt based on a fixed rate and payment amount.

Franchise Agreement: A legal agreement between two companies that defines the specific terms and conditions of doing business with one another. An example of a franchise relation is what exists between an original equipment manufacturer and its distributors.

Funneling: A technique for information gathering that involves asking more open-ended than closed-ended questions.

GAAP: Generally Accepted Accounting Principles. A widely accepted set of conventions, procedures, rules, and standards for reporting financial information as established by the Financial Accounting Standards Board (FASB).

Gap Analysis: The process of examining where you are in relation to where you want to be. In other words, the analysis process is to close the "gap" between actual and projected results.

Gross Profit: Gross profit is a company's net sales minus its cost of goods sold.

Gross Sales: A company's total sales before discounts, allowances, and returns have been subtracted.

Hit Rate: The author's term for the percentage of products booked, compared to the number of products quoted.

IT: Information Technology. A broad term that applies to all aspects of processing data. This includes all computer-related people, hardware, software, and networks.

Inventory: Inventory is an asset that is purchased by a company for use in the manufacturing of a product, selling, or consuming in the operation of the business.

Investment Banker: One who underwrites and distributes new investment securities. More broadly, one who helps businesses obtain financing and assists with mergers and acquisitions.

Item Class: A category of products that are similar in form, fit, or function.

Job Shop: See Contract Manufacturer.

Liability: Legal or financial obligations or responsibilities, including debt or contingent loss.

LIBOR: London Inter Bank Offered Rate. This is the rate at which banks and mortgage lenders can borrow from wholesale money markets.

LIFO: Last-In-First-Out. An accounting and costing method for a company's inventory. The cost of the newest (last-in) unit on hand is used when establishing the inventory at the time of a sale (first-out), and for valuing the inventory.

Manufacturing Burden: The overhead or operating expenses required to support the manufacturing of a product.

Master Schedule: The master production schedule that includes all material, outside processing, and labor required to complete a unit of work with specified dates.

Mission Statement: A statement of purpose for a project or company that generally addresses who, what, when, where, and why.

MRP: Material Requirements Planning. A mechanism to calculate what materials are needed, when they are needed, and in what quantities.

MRP II: Manufacturing Resources Planning. Involves the capabilities of MRP, plus long-range planning, high-level resource planning, master scheduling, capacity planning, detailed planning, and shop floor controls. One of its fundamental concepts is "closing the loop" and providing feedback.

Net Profit Margin: The ratio of net income to net sales. It is calculated by dividing net income by net sales during a time period and is expressed as a percentage. Net profit margin is a measure of efficiency and the higher the margin, the better.

Net Sales: Net Sales is a company's total sales minus certain types of returns, allowances, and discounts.

Net Worth: For a corporation, net worth (or shareholders' equity) is the amount by which the corporation total assets, stated at fair market value, exceeds its total liabilities on the balance sheet.

OEM: Original Equipment Manufacturer. This is a broad term that defines companies that add labor, material, value, and their brand name to products.

Open-Ended Question: A question that can't be answered with a yes, no, or specific piece of information.

Operating Expenses: The expenses required to operate a business.

Operating Income: See EBIT.

Operation: A specific set of production or manufacturing instructions.

Outside Processing: The service provided by one company for another company on parts being manufactured.

Order Fulfillment Cycle: The entire order processing cycle.

Outsource: To have a service performed or a function completed by others outside your company.

Pareto's Law: A rule that states that large numbers of effects are usually accounted for by a small number of causes, often the ratio of 80/20. The law is named after Vilfredo Pareto, an Italian economist who lived from 1848 until 1923.

Perfect Customer: A term the author uses to describe the attributes of a customer that allows the selling company to achieve controlled profitable growth over a long period of time.

Perfect Part: A term the author uses to describe the attributes of a part that allows the selling company to achieve controlled profitable growth over a long period of time.

Perfect Supplier: A term the author uses that is the same as the perfect customer, except it refers to a company's suppliers.

Points: This is the same as percentage. Two points equals 2 percent.

POU: Point-of-Use. A method of delivering materials from certified suppliers directly to where they are used in the manufacturing or assembly process.

Pricing System: The methodology or scheme that enables a company to establish consistent prices for their customers.

Prime Rate: The lowest rate of interest commercial banks charge large, creditworthy companies.

Pro Forma: A projection. A pro forma financial statement is one that shows how the actual statement will look if certain assumptions are realized. Pro forma statements may be either future or past projections. An example of a backward pro forma statement occurs when two firms are planning to merge and show what their consolidated financial statements would have looked like if they had been merged in preceding years.

Product: A part number or line item.

Product Line Manufacturer: An original equipment manufacturer (OEM).

Production Time: The manufacturing time, or "run time," required to complete an operation or a part.

Project Manager: The person designated and given the authority and responsibility to complete a project on time and within budget.

Quick Ratio: A measure of a company's ability to meet its short-term financial obligations with its liquid assets. To determine the quick ratio, you divide the company's liquid current assets (cash, accounts receivable, and marketable securities) by its current liabilities. The quick ratio is similar to the current ratio, but does not include inventory as a current asset. In general, a healthy company should have a quick ratio of at least 1.0.

RFQ: Request for Quotation. A customer's request for another company products or services.

ROE: Return on Equity. A percentage that indicates how well a company's common shareholders' invested money is being used. The percentage is the result of dividing net earnings by common shareholders' equity.

ROI: Return on Investment. The dollar amount of your company's earnings divided by the dollar amount of your company's investment, expressed as a percentage. For example, an investment of $1,000 earning $100 equals a 10 percent return on that investment: 100 (earnings) divided by 1,000 (investment) equals 0.10 (or 10 percent).

ROII: Return on Inventory Investment. The annualized gross profit divided by the annualized inventory investment.

S Corporation: A form of a general corporation that has special tax status with the IRS in many states. One of the attractions of S Corporations, in addition to the limited liability aspect, is the avoidance of double taxation.

SAM: Served Available Market. The dollar amount of products or services a company *can* sell into a marketplace.

SEC: The Securities and Exchange Commission. A federal agency that regulates securities laws, including the trading of public company securities, the firms that handle these transactions, and most professionals who provide investment advice.

Service Level: See Fill Rate.

Set-Up Time: The total amount of time it takes to prepare for an operation's production.

SIC Code: Standard Industrial Classification Code. A numerical system developed by the U.S. Bureau of Budget for the purchase of establishing unique codes for most establishments.

Six-Sigma Quality: This level of quality is plus or minus three sigma from the center line in a control chart. When used as a standard for quality, it allows for a maximum of 3.4 errors per million units or transactions.

Special Products: Non-standard products that are generally produced by a manufacturer on a when-ordered basis.

Standard Products: A designation of product established by the manufacturer for items they generally make, keep in inventory, list in their product literature, and for which they provide technical support.

TAM: Total Available Market. The total dollar size of a market that is available to a company for generating sales.

TQM: Total Quality Management. A system for continuously improving a company's quality that generally uses statistical process control, employee empowerment, and the principles of just-in-time.

TSR: Technical Sales Representative. A technical customer support person.

VAR: Value-Added Reseller. A broad name given to companies that modify a manufacturer's products and resell them to end-users.

Variable Costs: The costs within a company that change based on the level of activity. Examples of variable costs are payroll, travel, entertainment, and supplies.

Venture Capital: A mid-term to long-term startup or expansion loan extended to a growing business in exchange for equity in the business. Because the market potential of these companies is frequently disproportionate to tangible assets or other collateral, standard bank financing is often unavailable to them.

WIP: Work-in-Process (inventory). The uncompleted portion of material, outside processing, and direct labor in a manufacturing or contract manufacturing company's inventory.

Give the Gift of

CONTROLLED PROFITABLE GROWTH

to Your Friends and Colleagues

• CHECK YOUR LEADING BOOKSTORE OR ORDER HERE •

❏ **YES**, I want _____ copies of *Controlled Profitable Growth* at $24.95 each, plus $4 shipping per book (California residents please add $2.06 sales tax per book). Canadian orders must be accompanied by a postal money order in U.S. funds. Allow 15 days for delivery.

My check or money order for $_____ is enclosed.
Please charge my: ❏ Visa   ❏ MasterCard
                   ❏ Discover   ❏ American Express

Name _____

Organization _____

Address _____

City/State/Zip _____

Phone _____ E-mail _____

Card # _____

Exp. Date _____ Signature _____

Please make your check payable and return to:

BIZ-MANAGEMENT PUBLISHING
P. O. Box 1427
Pacific Palisades, CA 90272
Call your credit card order to: 310.459.5140
Fax: 310.459.1834
www.doucettecorporation.com